# Much MORE THAN THE ABCs

## The Early Stages of Reading and Writing

Judith A. Schickedanz

*A 1999 NAEYC Comprehensive Membership Benefit*

National Association for the Education of Young Children
Washington, D.C.

Verse on pp. 41–42: From *A House Is a House for Me* by Mary Ann Hoberman. Copyright © 1978 by Mary Ann Hoberman. Used by permission of Viking Penguin, a division of Penguin Putnam Inc.

*Photo credits:* Boston University Photo Services iv; Michael Tony-TOPIX 4; Marilyn Nolt 13; Robert Hill 18; Hildegard Adler 25, 89; Marietta Lynch 43; Jean-Claude Lejeune 46; Jonathan A. Meyers 52; Steve Takatsuno 55; Valerie Beardwood Kunze 72; CLEO Photography 75; Rick Reinhard 83; BmPorter/Don Franklin 95; Martin Deutsch 108; Renaud Thomas 117; Mary M. Langenfeld 124; Michael Siluk 136; Blakely Fetridge Bundy 147.

**National Association for the Education of Young Children**
**1509 16th Street, NW**
**Washington, DC 20036-1426**
**202-232-8777 or 800-424-2460**
**Website: http://www.naeyc.org**

Through its publications program the National Association for the Education of Young Children (NAEYC) provides a forum for discussion of major issues and ideas in the early childhood field, with the hope of provoking thought and promoting professional growth. The views expressed or implied are not necessarily those of the Association. NAEYC thanks the author, who donated much time and effort to develop this book as a contribution to the profession.

Library of Congress Catalog Card Number: 98-88656
ISBN 0-935989-90-0
NAEYC # 204

Editor: Carol Copple; Design and production: Jack Zibulsky, Sandi Collins; Cover design: Sandi Collins; Copyediting: Catherine Cauman

**Printed in the United States of America**

To the letter *A* for Adam.

Judith Schickedanz is professor of education at Boston University. She received her M.S. in child development in 1970 and her Ph.D. in early childhood education in 1973 from the University of Illinois at Urbana-Champaign. Professor Schickedanz has taught at the preschool level and has worked on funded projects in kindergarten and the early primary grades. At Boston University she serves as the director of the Early Childhood Learning Laboratory Preschool, which focuses on teacher education, the development of curricula and instructional practices for preschool and kindergarten classrooms, and basic research.

Professor Schickedanz is the author of numerous articles and several books including *Adam's Righting Revolutions* (Heinemann, 1990), *Curriculum in Early Childhood* (Allyn & Bacon, 1997), and *Understanding Children and Adolescents* (Allyn & Bacon, 1998).

# Contents

## Chapter 3. Preschoolers and Books: Contexts for Learning about Language and the World 41

## Chapter 6. Organizing the Environment to Support Literacy Development   135

# *Preface*

Over the years many preschool and kindergarten teachers have known that helping children get started in learning to read and write involves more than teaching them the ABCs. Many teachers of young children have also felt that, no matter how important a specific area of learning may be to a child's later academic achievement, nothing is important enough to risk snuffing out a child's zest for learning. "The teaching of specific things can wait," many preschool and kindergarten teachers have said. "We should concern ourselves with more important things, such as developing children's love of learning and nurturing their curiosity."

Twenty-five years ago I too thought about the teaching of reading in this either-or way, as if it were necessarily rigid and dull. I saw "reading programs" or "reading instruction" as having very specific components and a required scope and sequence. For instance, I thought a reading program invariably started with teaching children the alphabet, turned next to teaching children letter-sound associations, and then gave children words to sound out. Perhaps the program recognized the value of teaching children some high-frequency sight words and introduced them to new words before they were asked to read a new story in their readers. I assumed that comprehension would not be given high priority in early reading instruction.

With this conception of a beginning reading program, I considered it inappropriate to "teach reading" at the preschool and kindergarten levels. It seemed to me, for example, that teaching the alphabet would require engaging children in abstract, decontextualized, meaningless exercises. To my mind no good early childhood teacher would have anything to do with that!

I no longer hold that simplistic view. Direct experience with children, understanding more about the processes involved in learning to read and write, and thinking about what makes sense in preschool programs have all contributed to changes in my thinking.

My views began to change during the years I worked on a Right-to-Read project, a federal program designed to support the improvement of teaching reading to children who struggle more than is typical of most children with learning to read. A colleague in the Reading and Language Department at Boston University suggested that we write a proposal to obtain a grant. I remember saying, "Absolutely not! About the last thing I would ever do is try to teach 3-year-olds to read. They are not ready!" My colleague countered by saying, "The proposed guidelines do not require us to follow any particular curriculum or instructional program. We can do anything we want. Surely you can think of some way to approach reading and writing with preschoolers!"

I thought for a moment and then said, "Well, if I were going to do anything, I'd let children play with writing materials. I'd create a writing center, and I'd think of it in the same way that I think about a block area or a water table. I'd give children all kinds of paper and a variety of writing tools, and I'd let them experiment and play."

I thought my colleague would say, "Well, you will need to get a bit closer to bona fide reading and writing instruction than that if you expect a proposal to get funded." But instead he said, "OK, writing centers for exploration and play sound great, but we should also set up book corners in the classrooms and staff them with adults, such as graduate assistants, who will read stories to children." (My colleague's dissertation research was a study of parental reading to preschool children.)

Although I was very enthusiastic about emphasizing story reading in our proposed reading program—I knew that children who learn to read early have usually been read to by their parents (Durkin 1966)—I did not know just how central story reading is in helping children learn to read. I saw that, by providing opportunities for children to learn vocabulary and acquire information about the world, being read to contributes to children's comprehension. And I saw that hearing stories read enhanced children's enjoyment of books. But I thought the children in Durkin's study had learned to read through their parents' story reading only because they had some unusual talent for deducing letter-sound correspondences and the like. The possibility that reading to children—not the precocious few, but all children—would promote learning to read did not really occur to me. I considered my reading professor colleague to be very progressive in his thinking. "A good early childhood person," I thought to myself.

We wrote the proposal and received a grant. We went to work in six urban child care centers. Observing in the writing centers and book corners that we set up, I began to realize how much preschoolers learn as they participate in functional and meaningful literacy activities. The children often scribbled messages to parents, siblings, grandparents, and teachers. When they wrote in this way, they were very independent. At other times they asked an adult to write for them as they dictated a message. In these situations I found myself naming alphabet letters, pointing out patterns, demonstrating letter-sound associations, and describing how to form letters. I noticed that children watched and listened, often with rapt attention. Children also sometimes asked for specific instruction, for example, requesting that an adult show them how to write their name or how to form a specific letter, often the first letter of their name.

In the process of interacting with adults in these contexts, the children learned a lot about reading and writing. They even became interested in the alphabet itself. Sometimes they practiced writing a single letter, or they compared two or three similar letters, as shown in writing samples included in Chapter 5, "Young Children and Writing." I learned from the children that it is not necessary to choose between nurturing children's love of learning and curiosity, on the one hand, and teaching them about letters or other literacy-related information and skills, on the other. Such learning can take place in the context of broader activities at the writing center, as well as in art, science, math, and other learning domains, and in daily routines. When the alphabet is approached in these ways, children are as curious about it as they are about anything else they see in the world. It's just one more thing to explore, experiment with, and master.

As I learned more about what is actually involved in learning to read and write, it became clearer to me how very complex these processes are. They depend on multiple starting points and on a complex convergence and interaction of considerable information and many skills. A good oral vocabulary supports the decoding of print. Its use is not limited to the comprehension phase of reading, as I once had thought. The same is true of background knowledge and basic knowledge about language. We need to keep many balls in the air at the same time, *right from the beginning*. The alphabet isn't *the* place to start, anymore than oral language is *the* place to start. Starting on many fronts is important in developing reading and writing skills.

I have tried to capture this broader view of what is involved in learning to read and write in this new volume. Thus, the new name: *Much More Than the ABCs*. The title is not intended to imply that letter learning is trivial. The reader will find in this book much more than the ABCs as well as a considerably higher regard for the ABCs.

To accommodate the broader view of literacy captured in this new volume, an additional chapter has been added. The book begins with an introduction, "The Early Years: A Time to Begin." Chapter 2, "The Beginning: Babies and Books," is updated but resembles quite closely the same chapter in the original volume. The next two chapters are about preschoolers and books: Chapter 3 is called "Preschoolers and Books: Contexts for Learning about Language and the World," and Chapter 4 is called "Preschoolers and Books: Contexts for Reading, Props for Children's Play." These chapters contain a great deal of new information. Chapter 5, "Young Children and Writing," has been revised considerably to incorporate new information. Chapter 6, "Organizing the Environment to Support Literacy Development," is similar to the chapter by the same name in *More Than the ABCs*.

I suspect that many readers of the original volume began to outgrow it, just as I did. I think they will still feel very much at home with this new book. I hope that *Much More Than the ABCs* will do a better job of meeting current needs and will be helpful to preschool and kindergarten teachers as they work with young children in a variety of early childhood programs.

*—Judith Schickedanz*
September 25, 1998

## Reference

Durkin, D. 1966. *Children who read early.* New York: Teachers College Press.

Reading and writing, like other aspects of development, have long histories that reach back into infancy.

---

# *The Early Years: A Time to Begin*

I f people on the street were asked when children learn to read and to write, the answer most frequently would surely be "first grade." While it is true that most children begin to read and write *conventionally* while enrolled in first grade, these accomplishments are the end result of years of literacy learning (Leseman & deJong 1998).

Because only a small proportion of children, regardless of literacy experience, reach conventional levels of literacy before entering school, teachers and parents often do not realize how much experience children may bring with them to first grade. When children who are not yet reading when they enter first grade begin to read conventionally some four or six months later, the specific instruction provided in those months of school may appear to be responsible for accomplishing the whole job. But without a solid foundation of literacy knowledge and skill, children have considerable difficulty benefiting from the instruction their first-grade teachers provide.

Some children struggle in first grade to make sense of the instruction provided. Sometimes there is a specific difficulty standing in the way of an individual child's progress. When some characteristic of a child creates learning difficulties, it simply takes the child longer to make progress. But for many children—far too many—this kind of problem is not the source of their difficulty. Children who struggle with reading instruction often enter first grade without the foundation needed to benefit from the instruction their teachers provide to enable children to become beginning readers (Spear-Swerling & Sternberg 1996; Snow, Burns, & Griffin 1998). First-grade teachers know that when things go well for a child, they alone have not done it all. They wish that all children could get a good start with literacy learning long before they meet them in first grade. They wish there was more widespread understanding of the early experiences all children need.

## When do children begin to learn about reading and writing?

We all know that before children walk, they sit, crawl, and pull themselves up to stand. We know too that before children use mature speech, they coo and babble and then use holophrases and telegraphic sentences. We take for granted that motor skills and oral language develop continuously over a period of years. A long history of continuous development is typical in the area of literacy learning too, although it has taken educators and child development experts a remarkably long time to begin to think about literacy in this way.

### *Myths about literacy development*

Why did it take so long for everyone to realize that literacy learning begins years before children receive specific instruction in first grade? Why does it sound strange to many people even now when this claim is made? Some longstanding myths may have prevented our seeing that reading and writing do not simply appear suddenly at a single point in time but emerge slowly over the course of several years.

**Myth #1.** *Oral language must develop before written language can begin.*

Children are still in the process of mastering some of the basic aspects of oral language until the age of 5 or 6. For this reason, people once thought that written language development should not begin until after that age (e.g., Mattingly 1979).

*Evidence.* Although oral language development is essential to good written language development, it is not a prerequisite in the way once believed. Oral and written language skills develop simultaneously, with each supporting the other. For example, a good oral vocabulary helps children understand stories adults read to them and, later, stories they read to themselves. But children also learn many new words from listening to stories (Elley 1989; Adams 1990; Robbins & Ehri 1994). Similarly, sensitivity to the individual sounds of language, which develops as children hear and recite nursery rhymes and sing songs, aids in learning to read and write because it helps children become aware of the unit of sound represented by alphabet letters. Then, seeing the sequence of letters used to write words, such as the child's name or the words in a favorite book title, further increases children's sensitivity to the sounds that various words contain (Ehri 1975).

**Myth #2.** *Children learn oral language naturally, but they acquire literacy-related knowledge only through direct instruction.*

The belief that children do not learn about aspects of written language somewhat as they develop oral language results from misunderstandings about the development of *both* oral and written language. First, the experiences needed to support oral language learning have often gone unrecognized. Second, the beginnings of literacy development have often been completely overlooked or ignored. Ask parents when their child began to talk, and they give the age at which their child first used some well-articulated words, not the age when the child first uttered fully grammatical sentences. But ask parents when a child began to read or write, and they are reluctant to give the child credit until such behaviors match the conventional, or adult, models.

Because they overlook many of children's emergent literacy behaviors, considering them to be unrelated to later literacy behaviors, adults believe that children do not begin to learn about literacy until they get formal lessons in school. Thus, we tend to *over*estimate the extent to which oral language learning simply unfolds through maturation, regardless of social circumstances, while we *under*estimate the extent to which written language learning can occur in day-to-day functional contexts starting long before children receive formal instruction in the classroom.

*Evidence.* The kinds of social interaction necessary to support oral language learning have often gone unrecognized because parents and other caregivers talk to children in order to communicate, not because they are trying to teach their children to talk. Nevertheless, when we take a close look, we find that oral language does not occur without considerable interaction with adults or older children. If infants were placed in rooms with television sets but no responsive human beings, we would see how dependent oral language learning actually is on social interaction. Language develops when adults include infants and young children in conversation and when they treat them as conversational partners (Wells 1985; Huttenlocher et al. 1991; Hart &

Risley 1995; Huttenlocher 1995). In fact, tutoring is embedded in these interactions, as young children and adults communicate for a variety of purposes. Progress in language development is impeded, sometimes significantly, if children are not frequently engaged by adults in language interactions (Akhtar, Dunham, & Dunham 1991; Huttenlocher et al. 1991; Hart & Risley 1995; Oller et al. 1995).

The child is certainly predisposed—indeed wired—to learn language. However, it is misleading to claim that language emerges spontaneously in a child or that being surrounded by talk is enough. *Being included in talk and having talk adapted to your current level of talking* are required for optimal learning of oral language. Many adults speak to babies and very young children in a

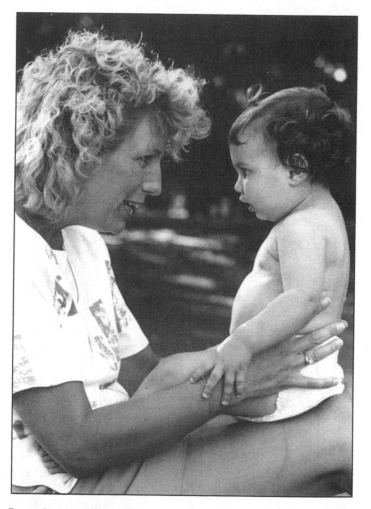

Parents and other adults who want to communicate with a
very young child typically adjust their speech accordingly.

way that makes language more salient to them and perhaps easier to learn. This special way of talking to very young children has been called *child-directed speech* (Fernald et al. 1989).

Children learn about written language in a similar, socially mediated way. This means that written language learning also depends upon interactions and that tutoring is embedded in these interactions. A great deal of explicit literacy instruction is typically provided to young children in context, often in response to children's requests for information and help. For example, when given paper and crayons with which to draw, children many times try to write their names. In the course of these attempts, they frequently enlist adult help. When adults respond to these requests, they often name the letters needed to spell the child's name, demonstrate how the letters are formed, and even relate the letters to the sounds heard when the name is spoken. Children also learn about the functions of written language as they observe and help parents make lists, write letters to family members or friends, or read menus in a restaurant.

**Myth #3.** *Children must achieve a certain level of physical and mental readiness before written language learning can occur.*

Some children mature early in the ways needed; others mature late. Variations in rates of literacy development are due primarily to individual differences in children's learning rates rather than to differences in children's early literacy experiences.

*Evidence.* First, in instances where considerable progress in literacy development has occurred before a child enters school, environments have provided children not only with physical resources but also with social resources—with people who give children information and demonstrations and answer children's questions (Durkin 1966; Read 1975; Teale 1978; Bissex 1980; Baghban 1984; Schickedanz & Sullivan 1984; Schieffelin & Cochran-Smith 1984; Schickedanz 1990; Schickedanz 1998). Teale (1982) explains the conditions which need to be met for literacy learning to occur:

> In one respect there is a literacy environment "out there" from which children might abstract features of reading and writing. Considerable print exists in the preschooler's world, and virtually every child in literate societies like ours has the opportunity to observe others reading and writing. But . . . children who learn to read and write before going to school do not do so simply by observing others engaged in literacy events and by independently examining and manipulating a written language. In an important sense the child's literacy environment does not have an independent existence; it is constructed in the interactions between the child and those persons around him or her. . . . In fact, the whole process of natural literacy development hinges upon the experiences the child has in reading and writing activities which are mediated by literate adults, older siblings, or events in the child's everyday life. (p. 559)

**Preschool teachers vary considerably in the ways they interact with children when reading stories.**

For many years, few researchers who were interested in literacy development looked closely at the interactions between children and adults (Hiebert & Raphael 1998). Instead, they interviewed the parents after a child displayed high levels of literacy development—usually when the child entered kindergarten or first grade. Researchers asked parents to recall what they did during the preschool years that might be responsible for their child's precocious literacy development (Durkin 1966; Read 1975; Price 1976). Parents often reported that they had done nothing in particular to help their child learn to read or write, although they typically recalled engaging the child in specific kinds of experiences such as story reading. They often reported that their children memorized favorite storybooks and then learned to actually read the words first in these, and then in other, books "all on their own." Because many parents are unaware of the learning they promote when they read a story, write the child's name on a drawing, or engage in countless other literacy activities with their children, the interviewed parents almost certainly underreported what they did. Their behaviors seem so natural and ordinary to parents—so much a part of their daily lives—that they do not even realize they are providing many informal literacy lessons each day (McLane & McNamee 1990).

These studies (Durkin 1966; Read 1975; Price 1976), and others like them, were misinterpreted for a number of years, contributing to the false impression that early literacy development is a natural development. Readiness to "soak up" literacy knowledge was in turn considered to be a matter of the child's maturational timetable.

When researchers actually watch parent-child interactions, or when they ask parents to keep a diary record of what they do to support their child's literacy development, a fuller picture of adults' role in children's literacy development emerges (Schickedanz 1998). Parents vary considerably in the extent to which they mediate print for their children and in the specific ways they do it (Scollon & Scollon 1981; Heath 1983; Teale 1986). Preschool teachers also vary considerably in the ways they interact with children, for example, when reading stories. There are specific consequences associated with these variations (Heath 1983; Dickinson & Smith 1994). Clearly, some ways of interacting with children are more helpful to them than are other ways.

Children who acquire a lot of literacy knowledge and skill before entering first grade are most likely to be those who have had a rich history of skillfully mediated literacy experiences. Children do vary, of course, in terms of the extent that they can benefit from specific experiences. Some children learn quickly from experience and thus need fewer experiences than do other children to make a specific amount of progress. However, the astonishing variations we see among children as they enter kindergarten and first grade seem to be due to wide variations in the amount and kinds of literacy experience different groups of children have during their early years. Opportunities for learning about reading and writing are simply more prevalent when children live in some circumstances than when they live in other circumstances. Parents with more education and greater financial resources often are able to provide more opportunities than are parents with fewer resources. Of course, socioeconomic and other circumstances do not necessarily define opportunities. Among families living in similar circumstances, parents vary in terms of literacy experiences they provide to their children.

## Goals of this book

Several years ago, when sorting through some old papers, I came across a piece of crumpled yellow notebook paper. When I opened it, I found this line of scribble:

Underneath the scribble, the child's mother had written:

> *Dear Miss Hoppin,*
> *Please do not get married. I want you to be the same old Miss Hoppin the way you are now.*
>
> *Love, Andrew*

Andrew was a 4-year-old in the preschool class I taught the year I got married. He wrote the note at home and brought it to me at school. As I looked at the crumpled piece of paper, I recalled many aspects of the original episode. I remembered receiving the piece of paper from Andrew and reading what Andrew's mother had written. I also remembered explaining to Andrew that getting married would not change me in any significant way.

I recalled, as well, that I was surprised by his confusion and touched by his concern that I would somehow become a different person after getting married (no doubt because he had been told that I would have a new name). But I did not recall thinking at all about Andrew's scribble writing. This aspect of the experience had totally failed to register with me at the time.

Thirty years ago, when the episode occurred, I didn't think that young children knew anything about writing. It was not something that experts in child development or education knew anything about. Years later, when I found the note, I knew more about children's writing because young children's capabilties were beginning to be discovered. Then, when I looked at the very same piece of paper, Andrew as a writer jumped off the page at me. I saw clearly what had completely escaped my attention before. Andrew had organized his scribbles to appear printlike, not picturelike. His dictation to his mother (telling her what the line of scribble writing said) took the form of a letter text, not the form of a story or a grocery list. If the idea of writing the note was Andrew's own—and I believe it was—he knew that thoughts can be saved for a later time if we write them down. And because Andrew never spoke about his feelings before giving the note to me, he must have realized that some things are easier to bring up if they are presented first in writing.

I wonder what else Andrew knew that simply passed me by. I am startled at the images that enter my mind as I think about that classroom. I never gave the children a chance to show me what they knew about writing. The only pencil in the room hung from a string attached to the easel. The teachers used the pencil to write children's names on their artwork so that they could later identify pictures and put them away in children's cubbies. Andrew's mother, wiser than his young, inexperienced teacher, made paper and pencil available to him. He also had four older brothers in elementary school. Observing them as they did their homework or wrote messages and letters, he probably requested materials so he could engage in the same kinds of activities. His mother or his brothers apparently supplied them.

If we have a restricted view about what early literacy behavior includes, and we have inaccurate concepts of how both oral and written languages are learned, then we are likely to believe that the onset of literacy skills occurs more abruptly and much later than research over the last several decades suggests. Even though most children will not read and write conventionally until the early grades, many have considerable knowledge about literacy and are well on their way to becoming conventional readers and writers by the time they encounter formal instruction.

This book is intended to help teachers and parents understand early literacy development and how to support it. It begins at the beginning— with a discussion about babies and books. It continues with a chapter on

> I never gave the children a chance to show me what they knew about writing. The only pencil in the room hung from a string attached to the easel.

preschoolers and books and then with a chapter on early writing. A final chapter provides suggestions for organizing a classroom's physical environment to support literacy learning.

The goal of the book is not to encourage parents and preschool teachers to teach children to read and write conventionally before first grade. Some children who have the kinds of opportunities described in this book learn to read during the preschool or kindergarten years. Others do not begin to read and write until they are in first grade. But all children benefit from the experiences that help to build the necessary foundation for learning to read and write. I have written this book to help adults give literacy learning a playful, interesting, useful, and joyous place in the lives of babies, toddlers, preschoolers, and kindergartners, at home, in child care programs, and at school.

## References

Adams, M.J. 1990. *Beginning to read.* Cambridge, MA: MIT Press.

Akhtar, N., F. Dunham, & P.J. Dunham. 1991. Directive interactions and early vocabulary development: The role of joint attentional focus. *Journal of Child Language* (18): 41–49.

Baghban, M. 1984. *Our daughter learns to read and write.* Newark, DE: International Reading Association.

Bissex, G.L. 1980. *GYNS AT WRK: A child learns to read and write.* Cambridge, MA: Harvard University Press.

Dickinson, D.K., & M.W. Smith. 1994. Long-term effects of preschool teachers' book readings on low-income children's vocabulary and story comprehension. *Reading Research Quarterly* 29 (2): 105–22.

Durkin, D. 1966. *Children who read early.* New York: Teachers College Press.

Elley, W.B. 1989. Vocabulary acquisition from listening to stories. *Reading Research Quarterly* (24): 174–87.

Ehri, L. 1975. Word consciousness in readers and prereaders. *Journal of Educational Psychology* 67: 204–12.

Fernald, A., T. Taeschner, J. Dunn, M. Papousek, B. deBoysson-Bardies, & L. Fukui. 1989. A cross-language study of prosodic modifications in mothers' and fathers' speech to preverbal infants. *Journal of Child Language* 16: 477–501.

Hart, B., & T. Risley. 1995. *Meaningful differences.* Baltimore: Paul H. Brookes.

Heath, S.B. 1983. *Ways with words: Language, life, and work in communities and classrooms.* New York: Cambridge University Press.

Hiebert, E.H., & T.E. Raphael. 1998. *Early literacy instruction.* New York: Harcourt Brace.

Huttenlocher, J. 1995. Input and language. Paper presented at the Biennial Meeting of the Society for Research in Child Development, March 30–April 2, Indianapolis, Indiana.

Huttenlocher, J., W. Haight, A. Bryk, M. Seltzer, & R. Lyons. 1991. Early vocabulary growth: Relation to language input and gender. *Developmental Psychology* 27 (2): 236–48.

Leseman, P.P.M., & P.F. deJong. 1998. Home literacy: Opportunity, instruction, cooperation, and social-emotional quality predicting early reading achievement. *Reading Research Quarterly* 33 (3): 294–318.

Mattingly, I.Q. 1979. Reading, linguistic awareness, and language acquisition. Paper presented at the Reading Research Seminar on Linguistic Awareness and Learning to Read, Victoria, British Columbia.

McLane, J.B., & G.D. McNamee. 1990. *Early literacy*. The Developing Child Series. Cambridge, MA: Harvard University Press.

Oller, D.K., R.E. Eilers, D. Basinger, M.L. Steffens, & R. Urbano. 1995. Extreme poverty and the development of precursors to the speech capacity. *First Language* 15: 167–87.

Price, E. 1976. How thirty-seven gifted children learned to read. *The Reading Teacher* 30 (1): 44–48.

Read, C. 1975. *Children's categorization of speech sounds in English*. Urbana, IL: National Council of Teachers of English.

Robbins, C., & L.C. Ehri. 1994. Reading storybooks to kindergartners helps them learn new vocabulary words. *Journal of Educational Psychology* 86 (1): 54–64.

Schickedanz, J. 1990. *Adam's righting revolutions*. Portsmouth, NH: Heinemann.

Schickedanz, J.A. 1998. Emergent writing. In *Theoretical models and processes of writing*, eds. L. Indrisano & J. Squires. Newark, DE: International Reading Association.

Schickedanz, J.A., & M. Sullivan. 1984. Mom, what does u-f-f spell? *Language Arts* 61 (1): 7–17.

Schieffelin, B.M., & M. Cochran-Smith. 1984. Learning to read culturally: Literacy before schooling. In *Awakening to literacy*, eds. H. Goelman, A. Oberg, & F. Smith, 3–23. Portsmouth, NH: Heinemann.

Scollon, R., & B.K. Scollon. 1981. *Narrative, literacy, and face in interethnic communication*. Norwood, NJ: Ablex.

Snow, C.E., S. Burns, & P. Griffin. 1998. Preventing reading difficulties in young children. Newark, DE: International Reading Association.

Spear-Swerling, L., & R.J. Sternberg. 1996. Off track: When poor readers become "learning disabled." Newark, DE: International Reading Association.

Teale, W.H. 1978. Positive environments for learning to read: What studies of early readers tell us. *Language Arts* 59: 922–32.

Teale, W.H. 1982. Toward a theory of how children learn to read and write naturally. *Language Arts* 55 (6): 555–70.

Teale, W.H. 1986. Home background and young children's literacy development. In *Emergent literacy: Writing and reading*, eds. W.H. Teale & E. Sulzby, 173–206. Norwood, NJ: Ablex.

Wells, G. 1985. *The meaning makers: Children learning language and using language to learn*. Portsmouth, NH: Heinemann.

To choose books for a baby or toddler, we need to know about what the child can do.

# *The Beginning: Babies and Books*

A boy sits on the floor looking at the book resting on his outstretched legs. He looks at a picture on one page, then carefully turns to the next page. Slowly he works his way through the entire book, then flips to the front to begin again. Unremarkable behavior, we might think, until we learn that the child is just 11 months old!

Although babies interact with books differently than do older children, even very young babies like books and engage with them in rather remarkable ways. This chapter is about babies and toddlers and how they interact with books at various ages. The chapter also includes discussions about how to organize a "book nook" in a group setting and how to read to such very young children.

## Matching books to a baby's development

If you were browsing through the children's section in a bookstore and another shopper asked you to recommend some good books for a baby, you would probably ask a few questions about the baby before answering. Among other things, you would surely want to know the baby's age and something about the baby's attainment of language and motor milestones. "Can the baby sit up?" you might ask. You might also ask if the baby can grasp objects between her thumb and index finger and if the baby recognizes and names any objects.

Before suggesting suitable books for a baby, we need to know something about what the baby can do. A book good for a baby of one age might not be suitable for a baby who is a few months older or younger. Knowing some of the characteristics typical of babies at different ages helps us select books for a particular baby.

## *Birth to 3 months*

**What babies can do.** Newborns can raise their heads for brief periods when they are lying on their stomachs. Gradually babies are able to keep their heads lifted for longer periods and can turn them easily from side to side. By 2 to 3 months most babies can keep their heads raised for quite a while when resting on their tummies. They spend considerable time looking around, especially if interesting objects are placed in view.

If held upright on a lap without support, a newborn's head will flop forward or to the side. Between 2 and 3 months of age, most babies become able to sit upright in an adult's lap and maintain good head control when support is given around their chest and trunk.

Everything looks a bit fuzzy to newborns and very young infants because their visual acuity is not yet very good. Newborns can see objects best when they are positioned about 7 or 8 inches from their faces. Although newborns can see no object completely clearly, even if it is positioned ideally, they can see well enough to notice patterns as long as the details are not too small. Several classic studies determined that newborns actually prefer patterned visual displays to patches of solid colors and that they prefer patterns with sharp contrast in brightness between the design and the background (Fantz 1963; Salapatek & Kessen 1966). A design in a black or bright, bold color set on a white background is typically of more interest to a newborn than is a design in a lighter color set on a white background.

During the first months of life, babies cannot manipulate objects voluntarily with their hands, even though they will grasp tightly a finger or other object placed in one of their hands. The baby's grasping reflex is triggered by stimulation of the palm. At first, objects grasped are not brought to the baby's mouth for exploration, but by 3 months the infant typically brings the object to the mouth to suck.

During this early period babies respond with rapt attention when someone talks to them, especially if the speech has elevated pitch, wide variations in pitch, long pauses, and exaggerated stress on syllables (Cooper & Anslin 1990). Speech having these and other characteristics is called *child-*

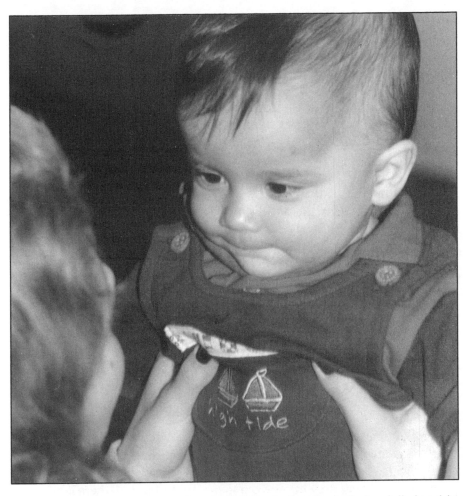

Infants are particularly attentive to the kind of speech that adults tend to naturally use with them—speech with elevated pitch as well as wide variations in pitch, long pauses, and heavy stress on syllables.

*directed speech.* Infants are very sensitive to speech adapted in this way, although researchers are not quite sure why infants like it so much or how such speech might help a baby learn language (Snow 1995).

As soon as they are born, infants begin to produce sounds. At first, they can only cry. By 3 months of age, many babies have added a lot of coos to their vocal repertoire. *Coos* are single sounds, with vowel-like sounds coming first. Babies become especially vocal when they are in a good mood—after they have been fed, for example. At such times of contentment, they often coo readily in response to someone who smiles at and talks to them.

**Books new babies enjoy.** At this early stage, a book must be something interesting for a baby to look at. The ideal book for babies from birth to 3 months has simple, large pictures or designs set against a contrasting background. The books should also be designed to stand up. Stiff cardboard books are usually a good choice. Some of these have connected, zigzag fold-out pages rather than single pages. This design feature makes it possible for all of the pages to be pulled out of the book's cover to create a long, colorful panel for a baby to inspect.

**Suggestions for reading to the baby.** Books do not figure very prominently in a baby's daily life at this young age. Eating, sleeping, and being comforted consume most of an infant's day. Moreover, because a very young baby's head and neck need considerable support when the baby is held, a parent cannot manage to also hold a book easily. However, books with bright, bold illustrations can be opened and displayed along the side of the infant's crib, to be inspected as the baby becomes interested. If the baby is placed prone on the floor for short periods while awake, a book can be opened wide and placed on the floor at a comfortable viewing distance.

Displays can be positioned so as to allow the baby to look only as much as he desires. A baby should not be literally surrounded by stand-up books, for example, such that by turning his head he cannot look away from them. Not all babies become overstimulated by bright, bold designs, but some do. The display should be set up to allow the baby to "take it or leave it."

This early period is a good time to introduce babies to language resembling "book talk" more than typical conversation. Nursery rhymes or other types of verse are especially appropriate. Because caregivers can recite rhymes or sing songs they know from their own childhood, there is no need to read these from a book. Young babies often settle down to the steady rhythm of such verses, which everyone appreciates! Over time, as specific rhymes and songs become familiar to them, babies' faces will brighten and break into a smile at the first sounds of one, as if to say, "I recognize that!"

## 4 to 6 months

**What babies can do.** From 4 to 6 months of age, babies usually become able to reach and grasp. Grasping an object is achieved first by folding the fingers around the object and pressing it against the palm. Because the thumb does not yet work in opposition to the fingers, the baby's grasp is awkward. At this age virtually everything grasped by a baby is mouthed. Mouthing is how babies explore and learn about objects. Babies also use their hands to bang objects on surfaces or wave them in the air.

Many babies can sit up by themselves around the age of 6 months or soon after. Sitting up frees a baby's hands and sets the stage for the baby to use his newly developed reaching and grasping skills to manipulate and learn about objects.

Cooing is well established by now. Between 4 and 6 months of age, infants add consonant-like sounds to their vowel-like cooing repertoire. Some of these coos, such as /w/, /p/, /m/ sounds (the diagonal strokes indicate oval speech sounds), are made by varying the shape of the lips. Babies also learn to vibrate their lips to "give someone the raspberries" (Oller & Eilers 1988).

Adults and babies can now engage in playful conversations. The baby makes a sound, and then the caregiver makes a sound. The baby "answers," and then the adult takes her turn. This kind of vocal play between babies and adults is common.

Language is both cognitive and social. Infants and toddlers attend to and develop language largely because they want to communicate (Bloom 1993). Social, vocal play during early infancy begins to lay the foundation for turn taking in real conversations (Bloom 1977; Snow 1977) and probably for the listening and responding sequences observed later when children listen to stories adults read to them.

**Books 4- to 6-month-old babies enjoy.** Cloth and soft vinyl books are especially good for this period because they are lightweight and compress when babies' hands grasp them. Thus, they are easier than a cardboard book for a baby to pick up. In addition, cloth and vinyl books do not disintegrate when they become wet, and wet they will be with so many visits to a baby's mouth! Another advantage of cloth and vinyl books is that they can be washed. This is an important feature of books when babies share them.

Simple, bright pictures set against a contrasting background still appeal to a baby at this age. Because many cloth books do not have good illustrations, especially if they're faded from repeated washings, it is wise to select only those with especially appealing visual effects.

**Suggestions for reading to the baby.** Now that a baby can hold her head up, a caregiver's hands are free to hold both the baby and a book. Parents who begin reading to their babies in early infancy often start now. But by 5 to 6 months of age, looking at a book without grasping it is a thing of the past. In fact, babies this age may look at a book very briefly. Instead, they grab books and then chew, suck, shake, and crumple them. In essence, a baby treats a book as she treats any other object—as something to be explored with mouth and hands.

A baby is most likely to visually inspect a book, rather than manipulate and taste it, when sitting in a lap. But even then he is very likely to bat at the book or grab it between two hands to bring it to his mouth to chew or suck. Sometimes a toy placed in the baby's hand will decrease the baby's tendency to grab the book the caregiver is reading (Lamme & Packer 1984). Giving the baby a toy to hold, chew, and mouth while the adult holds a book can encourage the baby to look at it. This strategy might be tried if the baby seems to want both to look at the book the adult is reading and also to manipulate or chew on something.

Babies continue to enjoy listening as adults recite nursery rhymes and sing, perhaps as they rock the infant to sleep. While the baby is awake, caregivers can recite nursery rhymes as a kind of play. Running fingers up and down an infant's tummy while reciting the rhyme "Hickory, Dickory Dock" is enjoyed by many babies by 6 months of age. Playing "This Little Piggy" with a baby's toes, while reciting the rhyme (perhaps while dressing the baby) also produces considerable delight. The babies' joy in hearing rhymes and songs tends to increase as babies become more familiar with them.

## 7 to 9 months

**What babies can do.** Babies are very busy at this age, especially if they have a lot of objects to explore. They continue to bang, wave, and shake objects, and they also start to drop and toss them. Infants can now easily transfer objects from hand to hand, which allows them to rotate and explore items more fully. They also can now hold an object easily with one hand while using the other to poke, pat, finger, or pull on it. At about 8 months of age, *deformation manipulations,* such as crushing and pulling or ripping materials, enter the baby's repertoire (Karniol 1989). All of these manual explorations provide the infant with a great deal of information about objects. For example, babies learn whether an object is soft or hard, smooth or rough, light or heavy, solid or filled with cavities, and tough or easily compressed or torn (Bushnell & Boudreau 1993). Of course, babies continue to mouth and chew objects, but these actions are frequently interrupted with fairly long periods of visual inspection and manual manipulation.

Near the end of this period, a baby usually becomes able to use her thumb and index finger to pick up small objects. This new skill is called a *pincer grasp.* The pincer grasp increases tremendously a baby's ability to handle objects. For example, it enables babies to skillfully stick a finger into or between things, such as the pages of a book. Babies can also begin to point at an object when they want it or want to know its name. An adult can identify the object that is the focus of a baby's attention and can name it. Frequent episodes of joint visual attention are positively correlated with vocabulary

> Babies' joy in hearing rhymes and songs increases as they become more familiar.

growth (Tomasello & Farrar 1986; Nagell 1995). Books provide wonderful contexts in which, by pointing, a baby can communicate clearly the object of interest.

Many babies begin to crawl by 7 or 8 months of age. They learn to pull themselves to a standing position soon after that. Exploring objects with the hands while sitting may take a back seat to moving about. Babies do stop for a rest now and then, and they explore objects during these interludes that punctuate their travels about.

Late in this period a baby begins to comprehend the meaning of words, even though most babies will not utter their first word for a few more months. However, *babbling,* or syllable repetition, is now heard when the baby vocalizes. Babies can say *"da-da-da-da-da," "ba-ba-ba-ba-ba-ba,"* and *"la-la-la-la-la-la."* Of course, such vocalizations have no specific meaning; the baby is merely getting better at producing sounds and at deliberately varying them. The specific sounds heard in a baby's syllable repetitions vary, depending on the language to which the baby has been exposed (DeBoysson-Bardies et al. 1989). Even specific patterns of intonation and stress found in the baby's native language show up in how the baby babbles (Levitt & Wang 1991). Research on babbling tells us that infants are very sensitive to the sounds of language and are practicing them. Research also tells us that the amount of babbling in which a baby engages varies dramatically and that this variation is closely linked to the amount of social stimulation, including language, the baby receives (Oller et al. 1995).

Late in this period the baby can search for objects hidden from view. If a 9-month-old baby has been playing with a ball and an adult playfully hides the ball under a blanket, the baby will immediately lift the blanket and grab the ball. Younger infants typically fail to search at all but look puzzled, as if they haven't any idea what happened to the ball (even if it creates a large lump under the blanket). Researchers now know that several months before infants respond by lifting the blanket to expose the hidden ball, they actually know that hidden objects still exist. Because they do not understand the spatial concept of *under,* however, they do not know where to search for an object once the blanket has been put on top of it. If, instead of hiding their ball *under* a blanket, an adult hides the ball *behind* a screen, babies 6 or 7 months of age search for the hidden object. Other task modifications reduce the need for the baby to sequence motor actions, which is difficult for young infants (Goubet & Clifton 1998). Apparently, even very young infants know that objects exist when they cannot see them. Because infants lack some spatial concepts and the ability to sequence motor actions, the classic Piagetian object permanence task fails to reveal fully what infants know. (See Schickedanz et al. 1998 for a discussion of recent research on infant cognition.)

**Books 7- to 9-month-old babies enjoy.** Late in this time period, babies' newly developed hand skills—especially their ability to use both hands when manipulating an object—allow them to begin to manipulate a book to look at its pages. The baby uses one hand to steady the book and the other hand to turn the pages. Stiff, thick pages are easier for babies to turn than are pages made of cloth or vinyl. (Cloth and vinyl books are so soft that infants find it difficult to wedge a finger between the pages.)

A baby's ability to handle and explore objects and his interest in seeing what objects will do make paper especially intriguing. Crushing, ripping, and the like begin in earnest around 8 months of age. Paper, of course, can-

Stiff, thick pages are easier for babies to turn than are pages made of cloth or vinyl.

not withstand crumpling, pulling, mouthing, and chewing. Clearly, books with paper pages cannot survive the independent play of babies this young.

A special type of cardboard book, known as a *board* or *block book* (and named Chunky or Chubby books by particular publishers), is fairly indestructible and especially easy for infants of this age to handle. These books are small, fitting rather easily in a baby's little hand. In addition, they are constructed so that the next page springs up as the previous page is turned, thus eliminating the need for the baby to separate pages that rest flat against each other.

Bright, bold illustrations of familiar things of interest and provide the adult with things to name.

**Suggestions for reading to the baby.** Caregivers holding a baby can now share a book with her for a longer time. Of course, "reading" a book to a baby this age consists mostly of labeling the pictures. Babies also enjoy hearing books with rhymes and rhythmic language, especially when these are familiar. Babies are not yet interested in stories in which characters with motives encounter situations and solve problems. Plotted narratives, as one finds in stories, are still entirely beyond the grasp of babies this young.

Because of their rapidly developing hand skills and ability to use their hands together, babies 7 to 9 months old may want simply to manipulate books. A baby may open and close a book, turn it around, insert a finger between its pages, help the adult turn over the pages, slap at the pages, grab the book and tap it on some supporting surface, and suck it. Some books should be available among the baby's toys to give the child plenty of time to engage in this kind of physical exploration.

When a baby is sitting on an adult's lap and wants to manipulate the book, the adult can let the infant take it. When the baby looks at it, the adult can label an object in an illustration and otherwise talk about the picture. If the adult holds a book out of the baby's reach, the baby may become frustrated and try to grab the book back again.

Adults must appreciate and respect a baby's way of interacting with books. Later in this period, usually by about 8 months of age, the baby takes more pleasure in looking at a book and less in manipulating and chewing it. Then the adult will actually have the chance to finish a book! Until that time comes, there's no need to force the issue.

## 9 to 12 months

**What babies can do.** During this period, babies become even more skillful in using their hands. By the end of their first year, many babies can place large pegs into holes, put rings on a post, and pull pop beads apart. Babies of this age are also adept at eating finger foods such as dry cereal and bits of soft fruit or vegetables.

Learning to walk is a major achievement for many children during this period. This new mobility enables a baby to get desired objects easily and to take them along while wandering about. Adults may find that babies now bring many objects to them. This is often the baby's way of saying, "Play this with me." When babies bring a book to an adult, as they will if books are included among their toys, it is their way of saying, "Read this to me."

Near the end of the first year, another milestone is reached: the child utters his first word. Babies this age also understand more of the words they hear—far more than the number of words they can produce themselves. Babies often comprehend more than 50 words, even though they are able to produce only one or two (Fenson et al. 1994). Adults can also generally expect appropriate responses to questions such as "Where is your nose?" Requests such as "Give me a kiss, " "Go get the ball," or "Let's find your shoes" are also understood by many 11- or 12-month-olds.

The first glimmer of pretend play emerges late in this time period. For example, babies may cuddle up with a favorite blanket, close their eyes for a moment, and then open them as they smile and laugh. They seem to be saying, "I was not really asleep; I was only acting as if I were."

Babies at about 1 year of age begin to make many connections between objects and events. When someone puts the baby's jacket on her, the child may say "bye-bye" and head for the door. When seeing a parent put on a coat, the baby may start to cry, realizing that the parent's departure is imminent.

Teeth are erupting during this time, and the baby may have an intense urge to chew and bite down on things. Drooling is common.

**Books 9- to 12-month-old babies enjoy.** At this time the book's contents, rather than its physical characteristics, begin to capture a baby's attention. Although babies still explore books physically, the contents begin more and more to dominate their interest. They now begin to recognize, understand, and relate objects and events in the world. Books with pictures of familiar actions and objects are the ones babies usually like best.

Cardboard books continue to be easy for children to manipulate because their pages turn easily. They must be selected carefully with respect to content, or they will be of little interest. If the pictures are not of familiar objects and events, the books may not have much appeal, even though their pages are easy to turn. Many babies are also skilled enough to manipulate the standard cardboard books. (The pages are thick, but they do not spring apart, as do the pages of Chunky or Chubby books.) There are many books of this kind from which to choose, although care must be taken to avoid the stories written originally for older preschoolers that publishers have recently begun to produce in cardboard page form.

Books with paper pages still cannot survive a baby's independent play. Although babies are now more interested in looking at pictures than in tearing pages, a baby's natural awkwardness in holding and handling a book will result in accidental damage. It seems that once a tear is started, a baby's attention is drawn to this activity and away from looking at the book. Before an adult can prevent it, a page has been torn out of the book and into little bits, many of which are likely to end up in the baby's mouth.

**Suggestions for reading to the baby.** When one reads to a child who is approaching his or her first birthday, it is often helpful to follow a particular language format. First, to get the baby's attention focused on a picture in the book, point to the picture while saying, "Look!" or "Oh, look at that!" Then ask a question such as "What's that?" or "What does that do?" or "What do you see?"

At this point the baby may vocalize in some way, smile as if recognizing the picture, or stare blankly at the reader as if having no idea what the illustrated object is. If the baby answers with a word, or even a smile or a gurgle, adults typically say something like, "Yes," and then give the answer or repeat the child's answer in a well-articulated form ("Yes, that's a monkey, isn't it?"). If the baby answers but mislabels the picture, the adult might say, "Well, it is brown like a dog, but that's a monkey. Monkeys have l-o-n-g tails."

In summary, the language format used when sharing a book with a child this age often follows a four-part sequence:

1. Get the baby's attention.

2. Ask the baby a labeling question.

3. Wait for the baby to respond or if necessary provide the answer yourself.

4. Provide feedback (Ninio & Bruner 1978).

The adult carries the dialogue forward in these episodes because the baby's productive language is limited. Ninio and Bruner refer to the adult's behavior as *scaffolding* (Wood & Middleton 1975; Wood, Bruner, & Ross 1976; Wood 1989). When we scaffold a situation for a child, we provide the overall language framework and fill in most of the slots in the dialogue. As infants grow older, they are able to participate more. For example, after several months of experience in which the adult points to pictures and asks the baby, "What's that?" the child begins to point to pictures and ask, "What dat?" Or, the baby goes through the book pointing to and naming pictures, even though her articulation may be awkward. Sensitive adults allow a child to take over the reading in this way whenever she can.

> After several months of experience in which the adult points to pictures and asks, "What's that?" the child begins to point to pictures and ask, "What dat?"

Many babies are now crawling all over; others are pulling up on furniture; still others are taking their first steps. Babies this age usually like to be on the move much of the time. Toys and books sprinkled about on the seat cushions of a sofa provide a play area for a baby who likes to stand but cannot do so without support. Babies this age also bring books and other toys to an adult, having picked them up from a toy box on their excursions. Adults can oblige the infant by opening the book and talking about the pictures on a few pages, although the baby might soon retrieve the book from the adult's hands and go on her way. Books can also be enjoyed in an adult's lap, usually at quiet times such as before a nap or before going to bed at night. If a teething baby wants to bite books and other objects, giving the baby a teething ring can decrease this tendency.

## 12 to 18 months

**What babies can do.** Productive language usually begins to blossom during this period. Babies are able to say more words and to understand more too. They like to name things, and they point to things they wish to be named. Children begin to use one word to convey many intentions. Their intonation indicates the specific meaning they give when using these *holophrases*. By the end of the period, some children are beginning to combine two words to form primitive sentences. They may also use *expressive jargon*. In this case the jabber is nonsense, but the intonation, stress, and pausing resemble actual speech. It seems that the toddler is playing and practicing with the overall rhythm and flow of sentences.

Pretend play becomes more common and takes new forms: objects are used for pretend activities, and dolls and stuffed animals may be taken for rides in wagons or rocked to sleep—sometimes after the child reads them a story!

Children this age might now enjoy children's television programs. They sometimes run to the set when a familiar theme song begins. Children might hum along with the familiar songs on these programs. Objects, animals, people, and puppets are often recognized on the screen, and babies may begin sometime during this period to point to and name them. A baby of this age will recognize and name stuffed toys made in the likeness of characters he knows from favorite television programs.

**Books 12- to 18-month-old babies enjoy.** Between 12 and 16 or 17 months of age children enjoy books with pictures of familiar characters (animals, favorite television characters, little children like themselves, adults in familiar roles), objects, and events. Because children this age are just beginning to sing, they sometimes enjoy books with songs. Books with repetitious verses may also be favorites, and a 16- to 18-month-old may jabber along as the verses are read.

Actual stories may begin to be of interest by 18 months of age. The stories must, of course, be simple, and should relate to characters, objects, and events babies can easily understand from their own experience. *Theme books,* the most suitable stories to read to a child this age, contain a series of related pages with pictures and a few words. A character might be shown eating his supper, having his bath, being dressed for bed, and then being tucked in, but no dilemma or problem is encountered; that is, the story has no plot. (See "Theme Books" at the end of this chapter for some titles.) Theme books provide a good transition between the earlier "point-and-say," object-naming books (one or a few pictures on a textless page) and simple but bonafide storybooks such as *My Blanket* by John Burningham.

**Suggestions for reading to the baby.** During this age period, children still like pictures in books to be named. They will repeat what the adult says, or try to, although their articulation of words will not be very accurate. Now they may be willing to listen to quite a lot of descriptive talk about the objects and events pictured in books. An adult can name an object (a cat, for example) and then, while pointing to the features, say that it is soft and furry, has a long tail, and has whiskers around its mouth. The adult might also make the meowing sound typical of cats and say, "That's what cats say when they want some milk." Many babies will look and listen to talk such as this.

Sometimes when looking at books by themselves, a child this age will jabber in a way that captures the overall sound of reading. This jabbering, called *book babble,* sounds different than *conversational babble* (expressive jargon), which children this age also produce. Occasionally, as the adult reads a highly predictable and familiar book, a child also may begin to chime in with a word or two if the adult slows down at opportune times to signal the child to join in. If nursery rhymes have been recited to a baby from early in infancy, they are well known by the time a young toddler encounters the verses in a book. Thus, reading nursery rhymes and other highly predictable text encourages chiming in.

Young toddlers are often quite physically active during book reading. Some of the activity may be an expression of excitement or thoughts the book elicits. For example, at 12 months of age, my son Adam became very excited when he saw a picture of a duck in a book. He was very fond of ducks at this time, perhaps because we made many trips to a duck pond near our home. When encountering a duck in a book, he usually climbed quickly down from my lap and ran to find his rubber duck, a constant bathtime companion. Or he walked through the house, saying, "duck, duck, duck," in a tone suggesting that he was very excited. Often he returned to my lap to resume looking at the book, unless he had found something else to do during his wanderings.

Older toddlers are more likely to stay in the reader's lap and express their excitement verbally. "That duck in the book looks like the duck I play with in the bathtub!" an older child might say. Older children are better able to make journeys in their minds and to tell us about them. But before babies can communicate in words, they must make the actual journey—they must get their toy duck, or they must move about the room repeating the relevant word ("duck, duck, duck"). Moreover, older children may no longer be surprised or delighted when they see something familiar pictured in a book. They now know that they can expect books to contain pictures of things in their own world. But a younger toddler, who is just finding out that familiar objects show up in books, is overjoyed with each discovery, and probably surprised as well, to see it there. The baby's intense excitement is often expressed through physical activity.

### 19 to 30 months

**What toddlers can do.** More and more, toddlers talk in sentences. At first their sentences are not typically well formed. That is, they are not complete in terms of grammar. *Telegraphic sentences* lack both whole words and parts of words used to indicate such things as possession and verb tense. For example, a child might say, "That my book," not "That's my book"; "Mommy purse" rather than "That's Mommy's purse"; or "Two boy play" instead of "Two boys are playing." A little later, when toddlers begin to form questions and negative sentences, they may at first misorder the words: "What it is?" instead of "What is it?" or "Daddy, no go" instead of "Don't go, Daddy." Despite these grammatical difficulties, toddlers' sentences carry a lot of information. In context, it is fairly easy to understand what they mean, even though they have some difficulty saying it. Adults usually find that they can carry on an actual conversation with a toddler.

When a child is between 18 and 24 months of age, parents often talk to their child about events they shared with her in the immediate past. For ex-

Adults usually find that they can carry on an actual conversation with a toddler.

ample, if the child goes shopping late in the afternoon with one parent, that parent might prompt the child to retell the experience to the other parent at dinnertime. At first the child may offer little or no verbalization. The parent then can ask questions such as "Where did we go this afternoon after I picked you up from child care?" If the child does not respond, the parent may prompt, "Did we buy some milk and bread?" When the child nods or answers "yes," the parent may continue by asking, "What kind of a store did we go to?" The child says, "Supermarket" (or some rendition of this, depending on his vocabulary and ability to articulate words). The parent can say, "Yes. We went to the supermarket and we bought milk and bread. We bought something else too. What else did we buy? It was something very cold. We put it in the freezer as soon as we got home."

Between 24 and 28 months of age, children become able to answer many more questions posed by adults about familiar and recent events. Between 27 and 30 months of age, children themselves begin to ask questions about recent past events, and they answer fairly well simple questions posed by their parents or other caregivers (Fivush 1991, 1994; Sperry & Sperry 1996; Miller et al. 1997).

The stories told when a person relates the settings, specific events (and their sequence), physical items, and people involved in past experiences are

> As children become more skilled in relating personal narratives, they begin to understand stories they hear in books.

called *personal narratives* or *autobiographical narratives*. The more that children are engaged by adults in this way, the better they become at calling to mind and relating events (Peterson & McCabe 1992).

Autobiographical narrative is similar in many important ways to the *fictional narratives* that children encounter in storybooks. At about the same time that children are becoming more skilled in relating personal narratives, they begin to understand actual stories they hear in books. Actual stories typically have characters and events in which some problem or difficult circumstance is encountered and overcome.

Narratives, either personal or fictional, involve people or characters and thus motives and feelings. Talk about feelings, their causes, and their relationship to people's actions becomes part of the conversation when caregivers and children discuss experiences they have shared (Dunn, Bretherton, & Munn 1987). At about 18 to 24 months, many children also begin to show empathy toward family members or others who are distressed, and they attempt to offer some comfort to them (Zahn-Waxler et al. 1992).

These language and social experiences begin to lay an important foundation for children's understanding of fictional stories. In plotted narratives people act because of reasons, or motives, generally based on feelings. Understanding cause-effect relationships in stories depends in part on our understanding of physical causality. (For example, spilling water on the floor creates a wet spot; ice on the sidewalk can cause a fall; snow melts when warmed up.) It also depends on our understanding of psychological causality, recognizing, for example, that anger sometimes causes us to do things we shouldn't or that when we have distressed others and we feel bad about it, efforts to make amends may make us feel better.

The child's interest in the physical world expands rapidly during this time. The child manipulates objects, often quite systematically. A child with a toy car might turn the vehicle over and spin each of its wheels with her finger as if studying how wheels work. Or a child might stack blocks in various ways to see the result. Even much younger infants know a lot about how the world works simply from having watched things happen (Goubet & Clifton 1998). For example, by 6 or 7 months of age, infants react to seeing an object apparently suspended in mid-air by extended gazing at the object as if puzzled by its not dropping to the floor (Baillargeon, Needham, & DeVos

1992). By 30 months of age, a child has gathered considerable information about the world, not only from observing events in which others are engaged, but from many hours of her own active manipulation and interaction with objects. By this age, a child is curious about why things happen, and the incessant "Why?" is often firmly entrenched in the child's verbal repertoire.

Pretend play continues to develop, and the child connects increasing numbers of individual actions into sequences. The older toddler, at 30 months, might feed a doll, take it for a ride in a stroller, and then put it to bed, even reading it a bedtime story.

At the end of this period, many toddlers graduate to a big bed and are introduced to a potty chair. The high chair might also be stored away. With the help of a booster seat, the child joins other family members around the table. The child eats foods eaten by the rest of the family, more or less, although a child this age typically resists unfamiliar foods. Autonomy, both physical and psychological, emerges in full force, although toddlers can also be very dependent. One minute they are sailing off on their own; a minute later they are holding tightly onto a caregiver's arm or leg.

**Books that toddlers enjoy.** Toddlers can enjoy actual stories now, and the events of a toddler's busy life provide clues about which stories may be of interest. For instance, they are likely to be interested in stories about messy eating, missing mom and dad when they are away, moving into a new bed, not liking a new food, or bumping one's head in a fall. Stories about going to bed, sitting on a potty chair, and leaving a favorite toy at grandma's house are also of interest.

Illustrations can now be packed with more information and action. Children spend a lot of time looking at the pictures in a book, labeling, making comments, and asking questions about the pictures. Storybooks intended for children this age often have a picture on every page, accompanied by just a small amount of text. Books in which the pictures are simple and closely linked to text appeal to children because they enable the child to relate what she hears to what the pictures show. Even older toddlers are not quite able yet to understand language well enough to get all of the meaning in a book

Talk about feelings, their causes, and their relationship to people's actions becomes part of the conversation when caregivers and children discuss experiences they have shared.

from the words alone. Looking at the pictures helps children understand what is being read.

Although stories are often of great interest at this age, active toddlers' urge to get up and move may make it impossible for them to listen to a long story. Sometimes toddlers play while a story is being read. Even when the child has delivered the book to an adult to read, the toddler might get up to play with other toys nearby. If the adult stops reading, thinking the toddler is no longer interested, the toddler sometimes returns to the adult and says, "Read!" Apparently, the toddler is still interested in listening to the book but also wants to be up and about, playing with toys. Fairly short stories work best under these circumstances. At night before bedtime, when children are tired, they often stay settled in a parent's lap for the duration of a story or two. Somewhat longer stories can be saved for reading at this time.

Toddlers love predictable books (see pp. 77–78)–that is, books in which sentences repeat, words rhyme, and pictures closely correspond to the text. These books allow for the full participation and autonomy of action that toddlers often enjoy. In addition, the older toddler's ability to sequence events and anticipate what will happen in a familiar sequence makes simple predictable books very appealing.

**Suggestions for reading to the toddler.** By the time a child is 2 years of age, he can take part in reasonably extensive "conversations" about a book, especially when it is about familiar objects and events, as books should be for children of this age. In much of this conversation, the adult is relating the book's contents to the child's life. For example, if sharing the book *Lily and Willy* by Martha Alexander, the parent might say, "Lily is carrying her doll Jane; Willy is carrying his teddy bear Teddy. You have a doll too, don't you? You have a teddy bear too, but it isn't as big as Willy's, is it?" On the next spread, where Lily and Willy are shown putting the doll and teddy bear into swings, the parent might say, "Oh, it says that 'Jane wants to swing,' and 'Teddy too.' You like to swing, don't you? We swing a lot in a wooden swing when we go to the park. Right? Oh, there's no bar in front on Jane's and Teddy's swings. I hope they don't fall out."

Looking at a page with a sprinkler squirting water on the children and on Jane and Teddy, the parent might say, "Looks like it's a hot summer day and they want to cool off in the water. We do that, don't we? Do you like to get wet in the sprinkler?"

The child often answers the questions and responds to the adult's comments. Some 2-year-olds contribute very little to these conversations; others have more to say. The adult must usually lead the conversation and actually does most of the talking. But the talking is done in a way that communicates clearly to the child that books can be talked about and that the child can contribute her thoughts and feelings. By addressing questions to the child ("You like to swing, don't you?" "Do you like to get wet in the sprinkler?"), the adult leaves openings for the child.

At first, the toddler might say only "yes" or "no" in response to a caregiver's queries. But in time the child will say more. By 2½ or 3 years of age, children often notice details in a book themselves and relate their experiences to what they see in the book. Of course, the extent to which children take this sort of initiative depends a lot on having had experience with an adult who modeled these kinds of "book-to-life" and "life-to-book" interactions. Parents and other caregivers vary tremendously in the ways they share books with children (Flood 1977; Dickinson & Smith 1994). These differences influence greatly how children themselves interact with books as well as the level at which they comprehend them.

## Book behaviors

Very young children differ greatly in all aspects of behavior; book behavior is no exception. Some babies between the ages of 5 and 12 months literally devour books. Others are content to look at books without taking them into their hands or mouth. Some babies sit quietly in a lap while being read to, seeming to enjoy simply listening and looking. Other babies struggle down from laps and stop by only for brief episodes of book reading in the midst of other activities. Some babies settle down to sleep with gentle rocking and nursery rhymes. Others fight sleep in general and would be stimulated too much, particularly in the early months, if adults recited nursery rhymes or sang to them.

How a particular baby interacts with a particular book at a particular time depends on that baby's style of interacting with the world in general, on the baby's past book-playing and book-reading experiences, on the characteristics of the book at hand, and on the general level of development the baby has achieved with respect to motor and language skills. Most babies probably exhibit behaviors similar to the ones listed in the four tables that follow, although each child might behave somewhat uniquely. Sensitive parents and caregivers watch the baby and try to adjust experiences and interactions to match what the baby can do and likes to do. In short, we must read the baby if we are to be effective in reading *to* the baby.

Information about very young children's responses to books is based on observations of relatively few children. Information about babies' responses to books comes from diary records, some published long ago, as well as others published more recently (Hogan 1898; Church 1966; Baghban 1979; Rhodes 1979; Butler 1980; Leeds 1983; Schickedanz 1983; Taylor & Strickland 1986; Morrow 1993). These lists of behaviors ("Book-

Handling Behaviors," "Looking and Recognition," "Picture and Story Comprehension," and "Story-Reading Behaviors") should be used as guides to observing children's book behaviors, not as lists of expectations for what babies and toddlers should do. The ages given for each behavior are approximations and indicate the range over which the behavior has been reported by observers. The behaviors are listed roughly in the order they appeared in the relatively few babies who were observed.

# *B*ook-Handling Behaviors

Book handling comprises behaviors relating to children's physical manipulation of books. The individual behaviors result from the interaction of a baby with a book, based on the characteristics of each baby. For example, a very young baby will typically maintain eye contact with the pictures in a book only when the pictures are simple, are bright, and contain a high degree of contrast. In the case of a baby turning pages independently, the ease of performing this action depends on such characteristics as book size and type of pages (e.g., paper vs. stiff cardboard), as well as the baby's age and motor skills. Specific book-handling behaviors are listed below.

1. Makes eye contact with the pictures but does not make hand contact. (2–4 months)

2. Grasps the book and brings it to the mouth to suck and chew. Shakes, crumples, and waves the book. (5–10 months)

3. Holds cardboard books, using both hands, and manipulates the book to make the pages open and close, exploring how the book works. (6–8 months)

4. Deliberately tears paper pages, when a book with such pages is offered. (7–15 months)

5. Helps the adult reader turn the pages, pressing the page to the left after the adult has separated it from the remaining pages. (7–8 months)

6. Gives the book to an adult to read. After one reading, often takes the book, hands it back, and requests that the adult read it again. (8–10 months)

7. Sits on an adult's lap or on the floor for extended periods (10 minutes or more) to look at books. (8–10 months)

## Sharing books with infants and toddlers in group settings

In group settings such as a child care center, family day care home, or play group, adults often consider how to make books available to children and how to read a book to an infant or a toddler. Babies younger than 4 months of age need to have books set in their cribs or nearby when they are awake and have been placed stomach down on the floor. When an infant is sitting upright on the floor in an infant seat, books can be set on the floor

**8.** Shows a notable decrease in physical manipulation of books accompanied by an increase in visual attention to books. (8–12 months)

**9.** May tear pages accidentally due to difficulty in handling books, but much less frequently tears pages intentionally. (12–14 months)

**10.** Turns pages awkwardly by herself, experiencing some difficulty in separating paper pages but succeeding through persistence and effort. (8–12 months)

**11.** Turns pages well. (11–15 months)

**12.** Flips through a book by gathering a clump of pages in a hand and letting them fly past. (14–15 months)

**13.** Turns an inverted book right side up, or tilts his head as if trying to see the picture right side up. (11–15 months)

**14.** Might continue to rotate a book in an attempt to get a picture right side up when something in the picture is actually upside down. For example, if a clown is standing on her head on one page and all objects are upright on the facing page, a rotation rights one picture but inverts the other. A further rotation reverses the situation, and so on. Because an inversion problem of this kind cannot be solved, the child may become frustrated and disengage from the book. (16–20 months)

**15.** Recognizes the difference between a book that is oriented incorrectly (upside down) and one in which a picture on a particular page shows something that is *intended* to be upside down (such as a sloth hanging from the branch of a tree). Does not rotate the book, or soon stops doing so, and does not become frustrated. (24 months)

# Looking and Recognition

This box describes how very young children attend to and interact with pictures in books and show recognition and understanding of them.

**1.** Looks intensely at pictures for several minutes, with wide-open eyes and thoughtful expression. (2–4 months)

**2.** Looking at pictures takes a back seat to bringing a book to the mouth to suck and chew. (4–6 or 7 months)

**3.** Hand-to-mouth manipulation subsides. Episodes of sustained looking at pictures are interspersed with hand manipulations and an occasional mouthing. (8–10 months)

**4.** Laughs or smiles at a familiar picture, usually when the adult makes an interesting sound or reads in an unusual way. (8–12 months)

**5.** Laughs or smiles when he recognizes a picture. (8–12 months)

**6.** Points to individual pictures. (8–12 months)

**7.** Vocalizes while pointing to a picture. (10–12 months)

**8.** Points correctly to a familiar object pictured when asked, "Where's the . . . ?" (11–14 months)

**9.** Names objects pictured (articulation may not be accurate, but parent or other caregiver can tell what the baby is trying to say). (10–14 months)

**10.** Makes animal noises or other appropriate sounds (e.g., *choo-choo*) when she sees the familiar animal or object pictured. (10–13 months)

**11.** Points to a picture and asks "What's that?" or indicates in another way ("Dat?" or questioning intonation) that a label is desired. (13–20 months)

# *P*icture and Story Comprehension

Behaviors in this box reflect babies' and toddlers' *understanding* of objects and events, not merely recognition of them, when these are pictured or described in books.

**1.** Relates an object or an action in a book to the real world (for example, goes to get his own teddy bear after seeing a picture of one in a book). (10–14 months)

**2.** Selects books on the basis of content, thus demonstrating some understanding of what they are about (for example, picks up a book with a picture of a duck after playing with a toy duck; frequently selects a book that relates to a significant event in the child's own life). (10–15 months)

**3.** Shows a preference for a favorite page of a book by searching for it or holding the book open at that page repeatedly, as if that part is particularly well understood or appreciated. (11–14 months)

**4.** Performs an action that is shown or mentioned in a book (for example, wants to offer the kitten a saucer of milk after reading about it). (12–23 months)

**5.** Makes associations across books (for example, retrieves a book about trains or gets two books and shows the adult that they contain similar pictures or events). (20 months)

**6.** Shows empathy for characters or situations depicted in books (for example, pretends to cry after being told that a child in a book is sad). (16–20 months)

**7.** Talks about the characters and events in storybooks in ways that suggest understanding of what has been said or read. Relates events in books to his own experiences. (20–26 months)

# *Story-Reading Behaviors*

Here we consider children's verbal interactions with books and their increasing knowledge about the print in books.

**1.** Vocalizes (unintelligibly) while pointing at pictures. (7–10 months)

**2.** Labels pictures in familiar books. (11–14 months)

**3.** Uses *book babble* (that is, nonsense jabber that sounds like the child is reading rather than conversing with someone). (13–14 months)

**4.** Fills in the next word in the text when the adult pauses, says the next word before the adult reads it, or reads along with the adult when a highly predictable text is read. (15–28 months)

**5.** Pretends to read to dolls or stuffed animals and to self. (17–25 months)

**6.** Notices print rather than just the pictures. For example, the child points to labels under pictures as the pictures are named. (15–20 months)

**7.** Shows some familiarity with the text. For example, says a word or phrase that goes with a page of text as soon as he sees the illustration (for instance, says "Hush" in response to seeing a certain page of *Goodnight Moon*). (17 months)

**8.** Recites part of a story's text outside of the story-reading context, for example, when swinging in a swing. (21 months)

**9.** Recites whole phrases from favorite stories if the adult pauses at opportune times. (24–30 months)

**10.** Asks to read books to the adult and may be able to recite several books fairly accurately, especially if they are simple and predictable (see Chapter 4, pp. 77–78). (28–34 months)

**11.** Protests when an adult misreads a word in a familiar, and usually predictable, story. Typically offers the correction as well. (25–27 months)

**12.** Moves a finger or whole hand across a line of print and verbalizes what the text says. The rendition may be the exact text or an accurate paraphrase. (32 months)

**13.** Reads familiar books aloud, rendering the text very accurately, particularly when a book is predictable. (30–36 months) nearby. It is a good idea to set some books aside especially for these younger babies. Books made to prop up easily are ideal.

Babies between 4 and 7 or 8 months of age are usually out of their cribs more but are not yet mobile. Books still need to be taken to them. Because children this age so often put books in their mouths, it may be best to set another group of books aside for use especially by this age group. These books can then be wiped frequently with a disinfectant solution.

## Creating a book nook

Older babies will enjoy a special book nook. Crawlers and walkers can get to an area where attractively arranged books are easy to reach. The typical upright book-display racks, so popular in preschool classrooms, are not very functional in an infant room. First, babies are not tall enough to reach the higher shelves. A second problem is that unseasoned crawlers and walkers may lose their balance if they must reach to obtain materials. Third, and more serious, the bookshelf itself can topple over if toddlers try to climb on it. (Furniture should, of course, be bolted or otherwise secured to walls or the floor.)

A book nook for babies can be made by standing some books up on the floor and laying others flat nearby. Because the opened and standing books can be seen from a distance, they will catch the children's attention. A corner of the room will serve best, as traffic will not go through the area. Make sure the area is covered with carpeting or a rug to make sitting comfortable. Pillows are not necessary in a book area for babies, nor are they very safe. Babies often don't watch the floor when they walk, and they are unable to raise their feet very far off the floor. (Were they to do so, they would lose their balance.) As a result, babies can trip over pillows. Moreover, a book is easiest for a baby to handle in his or her lap, while sitting. Leaning against a pillow or sitting halfway on top of one puts a baby in a position that makes manipulating a book difficult.

Although a special place in the room is provided for books, books do not have to stay there. Babies often get a book, look at it for a short time, and then carry it with them as they go to another area of the room. They might set the book aside while they engage in another activity and then pick it up again. Toddlers might be gently encouraged and helped to return books to the book nook when they truly have finished with them. However, it is good to remember that a toddler does many things while on the run. A book nook can be thought of not so much as where books *belong* but as a place where books can be *found*. If sturdy books only are provided (that is, books with thick cardboard, rather than paper, pages), they will

> Since they typically do things on the run, toddlers should be free to carry books with them as they go.

be able to withstand the wear and tear of traveling throughout the room with a crawler or toddler.

A book nook also provides an out-of-the-way place where adults know they can read to children without being in the way of other activities. While some children between 12 and 18 months sit quietly on a lap to look at books for extended periods of time, many infants enjoy books only for a few brief minutes at a time. They return periodically for several such episodes over a period of time. Of course, positioning oneself in the book nook will probably draw infants to it, and they might stay longer if an adult is there to share books with them.

Special understanding, patience, and sensitivity are required when we interact with babies and books. If we can learn to respond to babies' signals and to share books with them on their own terms, books can be the basis for many happy moments together.

## References

Baghban, M.J.M. 1979. Language development and initial encounters with written language: A case study in preschool reading and writing. Doctoral dissertation, Indiana University, Bloomington.

Baillargeon, R., A. Needham, & J. DeVos. 1992. The development of young infants' intuitions about support. *Early Development and Parenting* 1: 69–78.

Bloom, K. 1977. Patterning of infant vocal behavior. *Journal of Experimental Child Psychology* 23: 367–77.

Bloom, L. 1993. *The transition from infancy to language: Acquiring the power of expression.* Cambridge, UK: Cambridge University Press.

Bushnell, E.W., & J.P. Boudreau. 1993. Motor development and the mind: The potential role of motor abilities as a determinant of aspects of perceptual development. *Child Development* 64 (4): 1005–21.

Butler, D. 1980. *Cushla and her books.* Boston: Horn.

Church, J. 1966. *Three babies.* New York: Vintage.

Cooper, R.P., & R.N. Anslin. 1990. Preference for infant-directed speech in the first month after birth. *Child Development* 61: 1584–95.

DeBoysson-Bardies, B., P. Halle, L. Sagartt, & C. Durant. 1989. A crosslinguistic investigation of vowel formants in babbling. *Journal of Child Language* 16: 1–17.

Dickinson, D.D., & M.W. Smith. 1994. Long-term effects of preschool teachers' book readings on low-income children's vocabulary and story comprehension. *Reading Research Quarterly* 29 (2): 105–22.

Dunn, J., I. Bretherton, & P. Munn. 1987. Conversations about feeling states between mothers and their young children. *Developmental Psychology* 23 (1): 132–39.

Fantz, R.L. 1963. Pattern vision in newborn infants. *Science* 140: 296–96.

Fenson, L., P.S. Dale, J.S. Reznick, E. Bates, D.J. Thal, & S.J. Pethick. 1994.Variability in early communicative development. *Monographs of the Society for Research in Child Development*. Serial No. 242, 59 (5).

Fivush, R. 1991. The social construction of personal narratives. *Merrill-Palmer Quarterly* 37 (1): 59–81.

Fivush, R. 1994. Constructing narrative, emotion, and self in parent-child conversations about the past. In *The remembered self: Construction and accuracy in the self narrative*, eds. U. Neiser & R. Fivush, 136–57. Cambridge, UK: Cambridge University Press.

Flood, J. 1977. Parental styles in reading episodes with young children. *The Reading Teacher* 30: 864–67.

Goubet, N., & R.K. Clifton. 1998. Object and event representation in 6½-month-old infants. *Developmental Psychology* 34 (1): 63–76.

Hogan, L.E. 1898. *A study of a child*. New York: Harper & Brothers.

Karniol, R. 1989. The role of manual manipulation stages in the infant's acquisition of perceived control over objects. *Developmental Review* 9: 205–33.

Lamme, L., & A. Packer. 1984. Reading with infants. Paper presented at the annual conference of the International Reading Association, Atlanta, GA.

Leeds, S. 1983. A mother's diary. Unpublished mimeo paper.

Levitt, A.G., & Wang, Q. 1991. Evidence for language-specific rhythmic influences in the reduplicative babbling of French- and English-learning infants. *Language and Speech* 34: 235–49.

Miller, P.J., A.R. Wiley, H. Fung, & C. Liang. 1997. Personal storytelling as a medium of socialization in Chinese and American families. *Child Development* 68 (3): 557–68.

Morrow, L.M. 1993. *Literacy development in the early years*. Boston: Allyn & Bacon.

Nagell, K. 1995. Joint attention and gestural and verbal communication in 9- to 15-month-olds. Paper presented at the Bienniel Meeting of the Society for Research in Child Development, Indianapolis, Indiana, March 30–April 2.

Ninio, A., & J. Bruner. 1978. The achievement and antecedents of labeling. *Journal of Child Language* 5: 1–15.

Oller, D.K., & R.E. Eilers. 1988. The role of audition in infant babbling. *Child Development* 59 (1): 441–49.

Oller, D.K., R.E. Eilers, D. Basinger, M.L. Steffins, & R. Urbano. 1995. Extreme poverty and the development of precursors to the speech capacity. *First Language* 15: 167–87.

Peterson, C.L., & A. McCabe. 1992. Parental styles of narrative elicitation: Effect on children's narrative structure and content. *First Language* 12: 299–321.

Rhodes, L. 1979. *Visible language learning: A case study*. Urbana, IL: ERIC/EECE. (ERIC Document Reproduction Service No. 199 653)

Salapatek, P., & W. Kessen. 1966. Visual scanning of triangles by the human newborn. *Journal of Experimental Child Psychology* 3: 155–67.

Schickedanz, J.A. 1983. Literacy begins in babyhood: Notes from a mother's diary. Unpublished mimeo paper.

Schickedanz, J., D. Schickedanz, P.D. Forsyth, & A.G. Forsyth. 1998. *Understanding children and adolescents*. Boston: Allyn & Bacon.

Snow, C. 1977. The development of conversation between mothers and babies. *Journal of Child Language* 4: 1–22.

Snow, C. 1995. Issues in the study of language input: Fine tuning, universality, individual and developmental differences, and necessary causes. In *Talking to children: Language input and acquisition*, eds. P. Fletcher & B. MacWhinney, 180–93) Cambridge, UK: Cambridge University Press.

Sperry, L.L., & D.E. Sperry. 1996. The early development of narrative skills. *Cognitive Development* 11: 443–66.

Taylor, D., & D. Strickland. 1986. *Family storybook reading*. Portsmouth, NH: Heinemann.

Tomasello, M., & M.J. Farrar. 1986. Joint attention and early language. *Child Development* 57: 1454–63.

Wood, D.J. 1989. Social interaction as tutoring. In *Interaction in human development,* eds. M.H. Bornstein & J.S. Bruner, 59–80. Hillsdale, NJ: Erlbaum.

Wood, D.J., & D. Middleton. 1975. A study of assisted problem solving. *British Journal of Psychology* 66: 181–91.

Wood, D.J., J. Bruner, & G. Ross. 1976. The role of tutoring in problem solving. *Journal of Child Psychology and Psychiatry* 17: 89–100.

Zahn-Waxler, C., M. Radke-Yarrow, E. Wagner, & M. Chapman. 1992. Development of concern for others. *Developmental Psychology* 28 (1): 126–36.

# Books for babies

## *Books to prop up for very young babies to look at*

Bruna, D. 1980. *My toys.* Los Angeles: Price, Stern, & Sloan. This zigzag book is easy to prop up. The pictures are simple, with bright colors and a lot of contrast. (A number of zigzag books are on the market. Be sure to inspect the illustrations carefully. Several have detailed illustrations in pastels, rather than simple, bright, high-contrast illustrations of the kind needed by a young baby.)

Johnson & Johnson. *Visual display.* Skillman, NJ: Author. This book toy is constructed especially for propping up. It consists of two separate panels with three sections (pages) each. The sections can be folded and interlocked to form triangles, which stand up especially well. The pictures and designs are simple, are bright, and contain ideal contrast to catch the attention of a young baby.

Warabe, K. 1997. *Baby animals.* Tokyo: FlipFlop Books by Froebel-Kan. This is a zigzag rather than a bound book, which makes it easy to prop up in a crib or on the floor. A picture of an animal is on each page. Pictures are bright, bold, and high in contrast.

Warabe, K. 1997. *Zoom zoom.* Tokyo: FlipFlop Books by Froebel-Kan. Another zigzag book. This one contains bright, bold pictures of vehicles.

## *Books of rhyming verses and songs (appropriate for the infant from 5 to 6 months and older)*

Aliki. 1968. *Hush little baby: A folk lullaby.* Englewood Cliffs, NJ: Prentice-Hall.

Chorao, K. 1977. *The baby's lap book.* New York: Dutton.

Fox, M. 1997. *Time for bed.* Orlando, FL: First Red Wagon Books (Harcourt Brace).

Rackham, A., illustrator. 1975. *Mother Goose.* New York: Viking.

Rosetti, C. 1968. *Sing song: A nursery rhyme book.* New York: Macmillan.

Most children's bookstores and libraries have a number of good volumes of rhymes and songs. Look for one you like that also meets your baby's needs.

## *Books designed to withstand young babies' manipulation (cardboard, cloth, and soft vinyl books)*

Dick Bruna Cloth Book Set. 1976. *Dressing, Working,* and *Counting.* Toys To Grow On, P.O. Box 17, Long Beach, CA 90801. Cloth books with simple, vibrant illustrations.

Fujikawa, G. 1990. *Good night, sleep tight! Shhh* . . . . New York: Random House. A Chunky Shape Book (cardboard), with a simple text.

Greeley, V. 1984. *Zoo animals, pets, and field animals.* New York: Harper & Row. Cardboard, with beautiful illustrations.

*Looking at animals.* 1981. Los Angeles: Price, Stern & Sloan. Very colorful and made of stiff cardboard.

Miller, J.P. 1979. *The cow says moo.* New York: Random House. A cloth book with fairly good illustrations.

*My house, My yard,* and others. 1978. New York: Golden Press. Cardboard, relatively small, bright illustrations.

Tucker, S. 1990. *At home.* New York: Simon & Schuster. This small cardboard book shows one bright picture per page, including an apple, a crib, a cup, and a high chair. A Little Simon Book.

## Books with easy-to-turn pages (especially good for babies who are just beginning to turn pages)

*Baby animals.* 1983. New York: Macmillan. A block book with cardboard pages.

*Mother Goose rhymes.* 1984. New York: Simon & Schuster. A super Chubby book with cardboard pages.

Phillips, M. 1984. *Cats to count.* New York: Random House. A Chunky book with cardboard pages.

Ross, A. 1993. *Elmo's little playhouse.* New York: Random House. A small Chunky book.

Sesame Street. *Ernie and Bert can . . . Can you?* 1982. New York: Random House. A Chunky book.

Smallon, M.J. 1981. *The alligators ABC.* New York: Random House. A Chunky book.

Good books for introducing babies to the names of things (especially appropriate for the baby between 9 and 18 months of age).

*Baby's first book.* 1960. New York: Platt & Munk. Cardboard pages with several pictures to a page.

Bruna, D. 1967. *B is for bear.* Los Angeles: Price, Stern & Sloan. Paper pages; therefore, not suitable for independent play.

First Word Series, *Clothes, Food, Garden,* and *Kitchen.* 1996. New York: Snapshot Covent Garden Books. Four small books, with cardboard pages, including photographs (several to a page) of items belonging to the category indicated by the title of the book.

Fleming, D. 1994. *Barnyard banter.* New York: Henry, Holt & Company. Brightly colored rhyming text showing barnyard animals. Sounds typically made by each animal are built into the simple rhyme on each page.

Hooker, Y. 1978. *One green frog.* New York: Grosset & Dunlap. A cardboard book with an animal on each page. A bright, bold picture and a simple rhyming verse introduce each animal. Each page has a hole for the animal's eye.

Martin, B. 1983. *Brown bear, brown bear.* New York: Holt, Rinehart & Winston. A rhyming book that introduces many animals. Each animal is named and described with a color name. Paper pages, so not suitable for independent play.

Martin, B. 1990. *Polar bear, polar bear.* (Pictures by Eric Carle.) New York: Henry Holt. Identical in design to *Brown Bear, Brown Bear,* but introduces more exotic animals. Instead of color descriptions, a sound is provided with each animal pictured and named.

Oxenbury, H. 1985. *I see.* Cambridge, MA: Candlewick Press. A child sees common objects. Very simple illustrations.

Scarry, R. 1985. *Best word book ever.* New York: Golden Press. Paper pages with many pictures to the page. Not for the child younger than 1 year of age, but loved by many children older than that age. Provides many hours of pleasure for the child who likes to name things—or have them named.

Tucker, S. 1990. *At home.* New York: Simon & Schuster. A small Little Simon Book showing one bright picture (for example, an apple, crib, cup, and high chair) per board page.

Tucker, S. 1998. *Colors.* New York: Simon & Schuster. (A Nursery Board Book.) Each page shows an object, brightly colored. Simple text names the object and color ("yellow balloon"; "orange carrot").

## Theme books

Barton, B. 1986. *Trucks.* New York: Harper Festival. A cardboard book with bright bold colors that introduces trucks and the work they do.

Brown, M.W. 1996. *A child's good night book.* New York: Harper Festival Board Book. Small cardboard book that introduces an animal or thing going to sleep on each page.

Fujikawa, G. 1957. *Faraway friends.* New York: Grosset & Dunlap. Cardboard pages.

Fujikawa, G. 1975. *Sleepytime.* New York: Grosset & Dunlap. Another cardboard theme book. Nice illustrations.

Hughes, S. 1997. *Being together.* Cambridge, MA: Candlewick Press. Shows two children doing something different together on each page. Lovely rhyming verse.

Ross, K. 1989. *The little quiet book.* New York: Random House. A little Chunky Book that uses a simple rhyming verse on each page to introduce things associated with quiet.

## Books with simple stories (for babies just beginning to be able to sit long enough to listen to a real story)

Alexander, M. 1993. *Lily and Willy.* Cambridge, MA: Candlewick Press. A small cardboard-page book that tells about two friends, one with a doll and one with a teddy bear. On each spread the doll takes the lead in doing something, and the teddy follows suit. At the end, the doll wants to take a nap, but the teddy says "no."

Brown, M.W. 1947. *Goodnight moon.* New York: Harper & Row. Lots of repetition and easy to understand. A good story to read at bedtime.

Burningham, J. 1975. *The blanket.* New York: Crowell. A very short story about an object most dear to babies' hearts.

Carle, E. 1972. *The very hungry caterpillar.* New York: Philomel. Repetitious text involving many familiar foods and a caterpillar.

Krauss, R. 1945. *The carrot seed.* New York: Harper & Row. Paper pages and very simple text.

The children who make good progress in learning to read during first grade are usually those who enter with considerable book experience under their belts.

3

# Preschoolers and Books: Contexts for Learning about Language and the World

Books allow children to visit places for the very first time or to revisit places they already know a lot about. From their journeys in books, children can learn an amazing amount about many things. Books also help children to learn language and to learn to think about language.

Mary Ann Hoberman's *A House Is a House for Me* illustrates how rich books can be in possibilities for a child's learning. She starts her verse speaking of houses children are likely to know about and of the common meaning of *house* as a shelter for an animal, insect, bird, or person:

A hill is a house for an ant, an ant.
A hive is a house for a bee.
A hole is a house for a mole or a mouse.
And a house is a house for me!
A web is a house for a spider
A bird builds a nest in a tree.
There is nothing so snug as a bug in a rug
And a house is a house for me!

As the verse continues, the meaning of house expands to include anything in which something concrete resides:

A husk is a house for a corn ear.
A pod is a place for a pea.
A nutshell's a hut for a hickory nut
But what is a shelter for me?

And a little farther into the verse, the meaning of house is expanded still further to include places for things that are not concrete or tangible:

A book is a house for a story.
A rose is a house for a smell.
My head is a house for a secret,
A secret I never will tell.

The sound of the book's language provides considerable delight all on its own. It is rhythmical, even musical, given the conventions of verse used by the author. The rhyme and alliteration ("A nutshell's a hut for a hickory nut"; "And bathrobes and baskets and bins") make the listener aware of individual sounds of language in ways that ordinary conversation cannot. The tongue-twister quality of some of the text ("A pot is a spot for potatoes"; "Each snail has a shell and each turtle as well") causes the reader to slow down in order to enunciate clearly the words, making each one more salient here than when heard in ordinary talk.

The language is also jam-packed with information. Houses for different animals have specific names: hutches for rabbits, coops for chickens, sties for pigs. We learn of cartons and boxes, barrels and bottles, pots and jars, and of the things housed in each. We learn about vegetable and fruit coverings—husks, pods, and nutshells. We hear compound words: teabag, teapot, and teahouse; bathrobes; earmuffs; eggshells; and tablecloths.

The illustrations show each house mentioned in the text as well as some that are not. On the page where the text says, "The more that you think about houses for things, / The more things are houses to you," a boy is pictured lying in a hammock with his eyes closed. His thoughts about possible houses are pictured in bubbles floating around him. This page invites children to name the things and the houses that have come to the boy's mind and to think of other possibilities for houses and their contents.

When we consider all that a good book has to offer preschool and kindergarten children, it is not surprising that the children who make good progress in learning to read during first grade are usually those who enter with considerable book experience under their belts. Of all the literacy experiences children can have during their preschool years, storybook reading seems to be the most powerful in helping them learn language and gain knowledge about the world.

Why is experience with books so good for children? What exactly can children learn from listening to stories and retelling them? Is children's learning affected by how adults read stories and other books to them or by how adults talk to children about stories and books? What about the books themselves? Do the books we read to children affect their language learning and their interest and success in trying to read books themselves?

This chapter is intended to answer these questions. It starts with a discussion about the contribution books can make to various aspects of children's language development, which then is followed by a discussion about how books contribute to children's knowledge about the world. The topic of books as contexts in which children can practice all that they are learning about literacy by trying to read books themselves is saved for Chapter 4.

Rhyme and alliteration make the listener aware of individual sounds of language in ways that ordinary conversation cannot.

## Books and language learning

Researchers have found a very strong relationship between language development during the early years and reading ability in the primary grades and beyond (Butler et al. 1985; Wells 1985; Pikulski & Tobin 1989; Snyder & Downey 1991; Crain-Thoreson & Dale 1992). A strong relationship has also been found between experience with books during the early years and language development. Books contribute in many ways to children's language learning. They help children learn new words and how to interpret complex sentences. Books give children opportunities to learn to interpret language that is decontextualized (that is, language outside of here-and-now contexts; see the section "Storybook Experience and Overall Language Development," p. 54, for an elaboration of decontextualized language). Stories introduce children to language that is more formal than the language used in conversation, and stories also provide children with opportunities to develop a sense of story—that is, to learn how narrative discourse is organized. Finally, reading to children can increase their sensitivity to the individual sounds of language because the language in books is often organized to make individual sounds in words stand out and be noticed.

## Learning new words from books

As discussed in Chapter 2, the one-picture-to-a-page format of books designed for infants and toddlers elicits direct labeling of objects by adults. Adults often repeat a label several times as they point to each picture. This repetition provides a model of language for the baby to imitate. The ease with which babies can say their first words depends largely on their having heard sound patterns of words repeated frequently throughout infancy, their experience in playing with the sounds of language when babbling, and situations in which they were encouraged to reproduce words just said to them. Simple picture books designed for babies provide a wonderful context in which babies can both hear new words and try to say them.

By 2 years of age, a baby's budding ability to talk opens a new world of possibilities for talking about and learning from books. Although children are always learning new words from firsthand experiences in which adults comment on actions and objects and ask questions about them, books also provide a good context in which children can learn new words (Senechal 1977; Arnold et al. 1994; Robbins & Ehri 1994; Senechal, Thomas, & Monker 1995). In both real-life and book situations, children older than 2 years of age are less dependent than are younger children on explicit labeling of objects and actions. With their budding knowledge of words and sentences, children of this age begin to infer the meaning of new words from hearing

With their budding knowledge of words and sentences, 2-year-olds begin to infer the meaning of words from hearing them used in context.

them used in context, whether the context is real-life conversation or the text of a book (Sternberg & Powell 1983; Dickinson 1984; Nagy, Anderson, & Herman 1987; Beals & Tabors 1995).

Of course, inferring word meanings is not easy for a young child. How hard it is for children to infer word meanings from books depends on characteristics of the book as well as on how the reader reads the book and engages the child in it.

## Book characteristics and word learning

The meanings of words are far more likely to be picked up from the story-reading context if the words are used more than once in the book (Elley 1989; Arnold et al. 1994). The extent to which a word's meaning is illustrated in a book also influences the likelihood that children will infer its meaning (Elley 1989). Finally, word learning is enhanced when a word is meaningful and salient in the story, such as when the word is important to the plot (Elley 1989).

A good example of a word that is critical in this way is the word "quarrel" used by Leo Lionni in *It's Mine*. Early in the book the text states, "On the island lived three quarrelsome frogs named Milton, Rupert, and Lydia. They quarreled and quibbled from dawn to dusk." On each of the next three spreads, there is a specific episode of quarreling. Milton begins quarreling first, when he shouts, "Stay out of the pond . . . The water is mine." Rupert proclaims next that the others should get off the island entirely because "The earth is mine." Lydia then screams, "The air is mine!" A toad living on the other side of the island visits them to complain about the noise. He says that the "endless bickering" must stop. The word quarrel is so integral to the story that its meaning is not likely to be missed by a child.

The type of book being read also seems to affect the ease with which a word's meaning can be inferred. Expository texts (that is, nonfiction, information books) seem to lead to more word learning than do narrative texts. By their very nature, expository texts explain, define, and give examples of things. They also seem to elicit more discussion from adults, perhaps because, again, the books themselves are intended to convey information. Several studies have found that adults are less likely to define or discuss words they encounter when they are reading stories (narrative texts) than when they are reading expository texts (Pellegrini et al. 1990). Because a story moves along, it requires a performance from the reader in a way that an expository text does not. Although narrative texts apparently do not elicit as much discussion from the adult reader as do expository texts, adults can learn ways to enhance children's word learning without interrupting the flow of the story. (The next section reviews strategies for enhancing word learning from storybooks.)

The format of a book—specifically whether it is a predictable text—also affects children's word learning. Predictable books (see the list on pp. 77–78) are controlled-vocabulary, controlled-language books. For example,

By enabling children to learn some or all of a book by heart, simple and highly predictable texts allow them to take on the role of reader.

a sentence frame might repeat throughout a book, or a large portion of it, as in *The Very Hungry Caterpillar* by Eric Carle and *Mrs. Wishy-Washy* by Joe Cowley and June Mesler. By their very nature, controlled-language books expose children to fewer new words than do books without controlled language.

Highly predictable texts, moreover, do not provide extensive explanations or discussions of words they introduce. For example, at one point in *Mrs. Wishy-Washy,* the text says, "'Just look at you!' she screamed. 'In the tub you go!'" A book with a nonpredictable text might have followed these sentences with another sentence or two along the lines of the following: "She raised her voice higher than she had ever raised it before. And she made a noise louder than any she had ever made before. Her voice was so loud that it could have been heard over the bellow of an elephant or the ferocious roar of a mighty big lion." The listener would get a good idea of the meaning of *screamed* from this kind of detail. In nonpredictable books, cues to word meaning are often provided as actions and scenes are elaborated and characters are developed and described. In predictable books, on the other hand, this kind of elaboration is less frequent.

Children love predictable books, and these certainly have an important place in preschool and kindergarten classrooms. They allow children to learn the text of a book very quickly. When a text is known, children anticipate what will happen next, and this can increase their attention to a book as it is being read. Children can also begin very quickly to chime in with the reader on key words or phrases. They can even read along for the entire text if a book is simple and highly predictable—*Brown Bear, Brown Bear* by Bill Martin is a good example. Finally, in a fairly short period of time, children can retell the text of a highly predictable book verbatim as they look at the book independently.

Thus, predictable books help children begin to think of themselves as readers because they give them an opportunity to practice actually reading, albeit with emergent rather than conventional strategies. (See Chapter 4.) However, as Dickinson and Smith (1994) have cautioned, in considering the power of books to support the development of vocabulary and story understanding, it is a good idea to keep in mind that "a steady diet of books with predictable text may not be optimal" (p. 119).

Predictable books do vary, of course, in the extent to which their language is restricted. In *One Duck Stuck* by Phyllis Root, there is considerable variation in the words used, even though the basic sentence frames stay the same throughout the book. When the duck first gets stuck in the muck, the marsh is described as "deep green." After two fish attempt to free the duck, the marsh is described as "squishy, fishy." When the moose fail in their attempt to rescue the duck, the marsh is described as "swampy, chompy." When the

> Children's language development probably benefits from a balance of predictable and nonpredictable books.

five frogs fail, the marsh is described as "creaky, croaky." And when the possums fail, the marsh is described as "reedy, weedy." Moreover, each type of animal moves to the duck in a different way: The fish *swim,* the moose *plod,* the crickets *leap,* the frogs *jump,* the possums *crawl,* and the snakes *slither.*

Of course, the greater the variation in the language used in a predictable book, the harder it is for children to memorize. *One Duck Stuck* takes longer to learn than does *Brown Bear, Brown Bear.* Nevertheless, *One Duck Stuck* has enough predictability to allow children to join in when an adult is reading and to prompt independent retellings. For example, each time an animal fails to rescue the duck, the text says, "No luck. The duck stays stuck deep in the muck." After each failed attempt, the duck herself shouts, "Help! Help! Who can help?"

Children's language development probably benefits when their teachers take a careful look at *all* the books they read over the course of several weeks to ensure that they provide a balance of predictable and nonpredictable books as well as a range within the books of the predictable type. Taking care to provide a balance in the books read will benefit children's language development without diminishing children's opportunities to practice and play at being readers. (See Chapter 4.)

### *Strategies for increasing children's word learning from storybooks*

New words are learned best when encounters with the words cause children to engage with them deeply rather than superficially. Sometimes the text itself supports deep engagement with a new word, such as when the text utilizes the word a number of times or when it explains the word's meaning by providing examples. However, even when a word is used several times in a story or when the text provides explanations, the author typically does not use didactic teaching methods (that is, *direct* or *explicit instruction).* Rather, repetitions and elaborations of the word are integral to the telling of the story. This is why we say that children infer the meanings of words *from context* as they listen to stories. This way of learning the meanings of new words can be contrasted with explicit teaching of word meanings.

**Explicit instruction on word meanings in "real-world" contexts.** An example of explicit teaching of word meanings in the real world (as opposed to the world of books) can help us understand what explicit teaching is. Consideration of this example will set the stage for a discussion of how teachers can make word meanings more explicit as they read a story.

In the following example, a teacher is introducing funnels for the first time at the classroom water table. During the morning meeting, the teacher commented briefly about several of the activities available to the children for the day. This is what she said about the new water table activity:

> At our water table today, we have something new. We have some hollow, cone-shaped objects, which are called *funnels*. We also have a variety of plastic bottles and jars. Some of the bottles have very *wide* mouths—*big* openings at their tops. See, this jar is as wide at its *mouth,* here at the *top,* as it is at its *bottom,* the part down here. But this bottle [picks up a different bottle] is quite different. It doesn't have a *wide* mouth; it has a very *narrow* mouth— a *small* opening at its top—because it has a neck portion [points to the bottle's neck] like our neck [points to her neck].
>
> Now, if I want to put some soapy water in the wide-mouth bottle with a dipper, it would be easy [dips some water to show this]. See how the water just pours right in? I'm not spilling any water over the sides. This jar's *wide* mouth makes it very easy for me to pour in water from my dipper. But, now, when I try to pour water from my dipper into this *narrow*-mouth bottle, I have a lot of trouble, don't I? The opening is so small that I can't help but spill a lot of water over the sides. But a *funnel,* this cone-shaped object right here, can help me.
>
> This *funnel* is very wide at the top, which makes it easy for me to pour water into it without spilling any at all. The interesting thing about a funnel is that it gets narrower and narrower, until it ends in a little *tube*—this hollow cylindrical part, right down here [points]. I'm going to insert the end of the little tube into the narrow mouth of my bottle [does so]. See how easy it is now to get water into the narrow-mouth bottle?
>
> Funnels are great! If you'd like to experiment with funnels, then you might want to visit the water table this morning.

In this example, the teacher explicitly taught the meanings of a number of words (wide, narrow, funnel, mouth, tube, top, bottom). Sometimes she provided definitions (for example, *funnel:* "a hollow, cone-shaped object"; *tube:* "this cylindrical, hollow part, right here"; *wide:* "a big opening"; *nar-*

**Children may infer the meanings of words from context as they listen to stories.**

*row:* "a small opening"). She also pointed to the relevant features of the objects as she named and talked about them (mouth and neck of the bottle; top and bottom of the bottle; wide and narrow mouths). The combination of telling children explicitly what something is (funnel, tube, mouth, neck) or what a word means (narrow, wide) while also *showing* children what is meant is very powerful simply because not much is left for children to infer—to figure out from context—on their own. Explicit instruction involves making things quite clear to children.

Explicit instruction reduces the need for children to infer understandings on their own. Explicit instruction need not be primarily verbal instruction, without reference to objects; nor does it mean that children will be given limited hands-on experience. It is a *supplement* to firsthand experience provided to young children, as the example with the funnels illustrates.

Whether given in the context of a demonstration or as children themselves experiment with objects and actions, explicit instruction is very effective (as long as children are attending, of course). Explicit instruction is actually used quite often by teachers of young children, even though many preschool and kindergarten teachers think they provide no explicit instruction at all. They associate the term *explicit instruction* with having a narrow focus on very specific "academic" knowledge. Not having such a narrow focus but working to achieve many goals by engaging children in broad, hands-on experiences, many early childhood teachers are unaware of how much explicit instruction they actually provide.

If we consider explicit instruction to be *any kind of help that makes things clear to children so as to reduce the need for children to reach understandings by inferring them on their own,* then we can see that many preschool and kindergarten teachers provide a great deal of explicit instruction. To be sure, they do not rely on it entirely. In fact, they probably do not rely on it primarily. The teacher who introduced funnels provided experience at the water table for children to experiment with funnels and bottles not only on this day, but for five days. Thus, children in this classroom had an opportunity to come to know very thoroughly what their teacher had merely (but very skillfully) introduced to them in a three- to four-minute demonstration. With young children especially, explicit instruction should not by any means carry the whole load of teaching. But slipping it in as other purposes are accomplished often helps children tremendously.

It is very likely that the teacher who introduced the funnels at meeting time had not even thought about teaching word meanings. Knowing that a teacher would not be assigned to supervise the water table area all of the time during the morning activity period, she might have been making things clear at meeting time because she wanted children to have a little information about what they would find at the water table and what they might do with the new materials. Perhaps she had noticed through her years of teaching that children are more focused and productive in their experimentation with new materials when they have some idea of what they can do with them. No matter what her primary purpose for providing the demonstration and the accompanying commentary, this teacher did a beautiful job of using explicit instruction to teach word meanings to children.

**Explicit instruction on word meanings in the story-reading context.** Teachers can use several strategies to make the meanings of words clearer when children encounter them in stories. In picture books, the type of storybooks typically read to preschool and kindergarten children, almost everything named and described in the text is illustrated. The illustrations in a book can be thought of as substitutes for, or representations of, real objects and actions. By pointing to the illustrations at key times as they read the story, teachers can help the illustrations do their job—to make the text more understandable to young children.

Thus, on the spread on which we find the text, "A husk is a house for a corn ear. / A pod is a place for a pea. / A nutshell's a hut for a hickory nut. / But what is a shelter for me?" in *A House Is a House for Me,* we see a basket of ears of corn in their husks, a bowl of peas in their pods, and a bowl of nuts in their shells. Children might not know one food from another, particularly when they are shown in their just-harvested form. By pointing quickly to each picture as the text is read, the teacher can help children link specific words (husk and corn ear; pod and pea; nutshell and hickory nut) and meanings.

Pointing to an illustration can be helpful not only when a number of items named in the text are pictured on the same page, but also when one item mentioned is set in its context, which may be a complex scene. For example, on the page in Hoberman's book where the verse reads, "A dock or a slip is a house for a ship," the dock, a rowboat, a ship, a whale, and a boy holding a boot and a fish are all shown in the picture. By pointing to the dock itself, the teacher can help children find the specific object ("a dock or a slip") to which the text refers.

When using illustrations in this way—especially when reading a book written in verse—stopping to point out word meanings detracts from the pleasures of hearing the rhythm and rhyme. For example, it is not necessary for the teacher to stop after reading, "A dock or a slip is a house for a ship," and say, "Okay. Now right here in this picture we can see a large wooden structure. The rowboat, over here, and the ship, over here, are tied up to this large wooden structure. This structure is called a 'dock' or a 'slip'; that's what we call the thing a boat or a ship is tied to so that it won't go floating out into the water." Instead, the teacher can simply point to the relevant illustration *as* she reads the text. This approach allows the verse to flow unbroken.

By pointing to pictures as they are referred to in the text, the teacher helps children link specific words and meaning.

*After* reading the entire book, the teacher can go back to several pages that she has selected beforehand to talk about specifically. For example, returning to the page with the slip or dock, she might say, "I see here a boy walking on the dock, and he has some things in his hands. I think this is a boot, and this looks like a fish. I wonder where he got these?" There would be some discussion about fishing and about the things, both expected and unexpected, one is likely to catch. The teacher might be able to work into the discussion a comment about the boats tied to the dock and how tying them keeps them from floating away into the lake or river. "The boy might want to go fishing again," the teacher might explain. "He'll want to find his boat waiting for him. How would he find his boat if it left by itself, floating on the waves?"

Teachers can also facilitate children's word learning from storybooks if they insert a brief explanation or a synonym for the word right after coming across it in the text. For example, in Maurice Sendak's *Where the Wild Things Are,* Max cries, "Let the wild rumpus start." The teacher might say, "It sounds like there's going to be a loud party. A rumpus is kind of a loud and boisterous party, something with a lot of commotion." When the teacher turns the page, exposing the first spread with no words, she can say, "I see that everybody's mouth is open. Looks like they might be making some noise." As she turns to the next spread, she might say, "Oh, now they are . . . " (pausing to let children fill in; children will probably say, "hanging on trees" or "climbing trees"). The teacher might follow by saying, "Yes, this sure does look like a *rumpus,* like a wild and noisy kind of party. Looks like they are having a very good time." In books structured differently (with no wordless pages following the introduction of a new word), the teacher simply inserts a *brief* definition to explain the word's meaning and then moves on.

During the first reading of a new book, teachers will want to be selective, picking out only a few words to explain. The words that are most important in helping children understand the story can be briefly explained the first time through. Teachers can then define a few words each time they read the book over the course of several days or weeks.

A third strategy for communicating word meaning can be used with certain words. In *The Very Hungry Caterpillar,* for example, the text says, "One Sunday morning the warm sun came up and–pop!–out of the egg came a tiny and very hungry caterpillar." The meaning of the word *pop* can be conveyed quite well if the teacher reads the word in a popping sort of way. When the teacher reads Ezra Jack Keats's *The Snowy Day,* she can use a similar approach on the pages where Peter finds a stick good for "smacking" snow covering the branches of a tree and where the snow goes "plop" on Peter's head. This strategy uses *onomatopoeia,* which refers to using a word whose pronunciation approximates the sound made when the action is performed.

Researchers have found that these three approaches to conveying word meanings in story reading considerably increase children's learning of new words (Elley 1989; Dickinson & Smith 1994). Teachers must use the strategies skillfully, of course. In addition to not explaining too many words in any one reading, teachers should not quiz children after providing information about word meaning, saying, for instance, "Now, what did I say *rumpus* meant?"

In one study, extensive use of quizzing in reading stories (that is, stopping to ask children literal questions about what was just said in the text or by the teacher) hindered children's comprehension (Dickinson & Smith 1994). Thus, the strategies described here should be used naturally, in the spirit of wanting to help children understand the story. These comments, gestures, and expressions should make the story easier for the children to understand and thus more enjoyable.

## Storybook experience and overall language development

It has long been known that children with a history of listening to stories during the early years have better developed language skills and better reading comprehension than do children without such a history (Chomsky 1972; Moerk 1985; Wells 1985). Of course, parents who read to their children may also talk more to their children than do other parents. Simply talking more with children helps language develop. But books also provide a model of fairly complex decontextualized language.

When we say that language is *decontextualized,* we mean that the person talking—the author in this case—is not face-to-face with the reader, and that the people, actions, and events occurring in the book are not happening right now in the child's presence (Ricard & Snow 1990; Snow 1991). Language must convey more of the meaning when a child is listening to a story and lacks the contextual cues of an ongoing shared event. To understand what is happening in a story, the child must focus on the language more than he needs to in real-life contexts, and this may promote language learning.

A history of story-reading experience might also be associated with good language development because a story has the potential to prompt considerable discussion. Simply talking —and hearing lots of talk from adults—promotes children's language learning. Even more language learning occurs when adults recast and expand children's utterances, which they often do as they talk with children in any context (Farrar 1990; Moerk 1991; Morgan, Bonamo, & Travis 1995). Perhaps more of this sort of adult responding occurs in story-reading than in other situations, at least when stories are fairly complex. Adults often find they need to clarify or probe what children are trying to convey in comments about stories.

For example, after a teacher read *The Snowy Day* to a group of 4-year-olds, one child, referring to the last page, said, "Oh, now Peter is bigger." The teacher did not understand his comment: "What do you mean Peter is bigger?" The child explained, "He can play snowballs now." "Oh," the teacher said, "are you thinking that Peter's friend was one of the big kids throwing snowballs in the story?" (The teacher turned back to the page.) "Yes," the child replied. "Oh, I see, he was alone before—not with the other big kids. But," the teacher continued, "I think this is a friend who is Peter's age and size. He and Peter still are too young to play snowballs with the big kids."

Researchers have found that parents vary a great deal in how they talk with children about stories and have determined that these variations matter. The more adults talk with children about the stories they read, the more the story reading helps the child's language development. In some studies, parents were taught specific strategies to use when talking with children about

Hearing lots of talk from adults promotes children's language learning.

books (Whitehurst et al. 1988; Arnold et al. 1994). The language of children whose parents received the training developed more optimally than did the language of the children whose parents read as many books to them but did not engage them in as much conversation. The power of the story-reading experience to influence a child's language development and story comprehension depends a lot on the kinds of conversation that take place during and after the story is read. Parents who answer children's questions, ask questions, and follow up the child's comments help children get the most out of the story-reading experience.

Some preschool teachers talk to children in a particularly effective way in the story-reading context. They use what has been called *cognitively challenging talk* (Dickinson & Smith 1994). This kind of talk is associated with higher levels of language development and story comprehension than is less challenging talk. Teachers who use cognitively challenging talk tend to help children analyze characters and events, engage children in predicting events, help children make connections between story events and real life, explain vocabulary, and summarize portions of the text after it has been read. They also ask children for evaluative comments such as whether they liked a particular part of the story and why.

When a teacher is reading aloud, much of the talking can take place *after* she's read through the story once, when she and the children go back through the book to reconstruct and discuss the story. It is helpful to know that talking about a book can be saved until the end, because many teachers of preschool and kindergarten children know that getting through a story is hard if there is a lot of discussion during the first reading. Children frequently go off on tangents, and teachers find that it sometimes takes a while to get back to reading the story. These breaks cause other children to lose interest in the book. The flow of the story is spoiled by starting and stopping. After a story has been read and the children and the teacher are going back over it, comments and questions are not an interruption, because the story has been finished.

In addition to generally helping children to develop oral language, exposure to books familiarizes children with book language. The language found in books differs significantly from the language found in conversation: it is more formal, and more information and images are packed into its sentences. Consider the following text, taken from Leo Lionni's book *It's Mine,* a story about three quarrelsome frogs who finally grow to appreciate each other:

> There was only one rock left and there the frogs huddled, trembling from the cold and fright. But they felt better now that they were together, sharing the same fears and hopes. Little by little the flood subsided. The rain fell gently and then stopped altogether.

If we were relating to a friend a personal experience of having been stranded on an island with water rising after a heavy rainstorm, we might tell it like this:

It rained and rained. You just wouldn't have believed it. The water just kept rising. Finally we were down to about one small piece of land in the middle of the island. It was about the size of that table over there. No bigger, I'm telling you. We were so cold and so scared that we were shaking. We just kept thinking, "Well, at least we are together in this awful predicament." Thank goodness, the rain finally stopped, and the water started going down.

There is more detail in the face-to-face account, and a reference to something in the room is used to help explain a particular situation the person was trying to relate. Instead of implying that they were all thinking about the same fears, the person giving the face-to-face account said, "We just kept thinking," and then related exactly the shared thought. In real life, listeners are also very likely to interrupt the speaker to ask questions: "How fast did the water rise?" or "Did you have any warning?" or "Were there any tall trees to climb?" As Holdaway (1979) has noted,

Normal spoken language is . . . a kind of composite message coming from language in association with sensory context . . . spoken language structures may be incomplete or ambiguous in themselves without being confusing. (p. 54)

Written language, on the other hand, cannot be understood by observing real contexts or by asking questions of the speaker. Because of its unique circumstance,

Written language . . . must carry the total load of meaning without ambiguity. . . . It is more formal, more complete, and more textured than spoken language, and to avoid ambiguity it has distinctive structures which do not appear in spoken dialects. (Holdaway 1979, 54)

## Book experience and the development of text structure knowledge

Stories (*narrative texts*) have a specific organization. Events and characters' actions occur in a particular sequence, in specific settings. Characters find themselves in predicaments. They overcome their problems by taking action, which is guided by motives. Thus, stories involve psychological as well as physical causation (Applebee 1978; Stein 1988). The structure of stories—the way they are organized—is called *story grammar*. Each story's specific structure can be plotted in a *story map*. The story map of *The Three Little Pigs* (pp. 58–59) is an example.

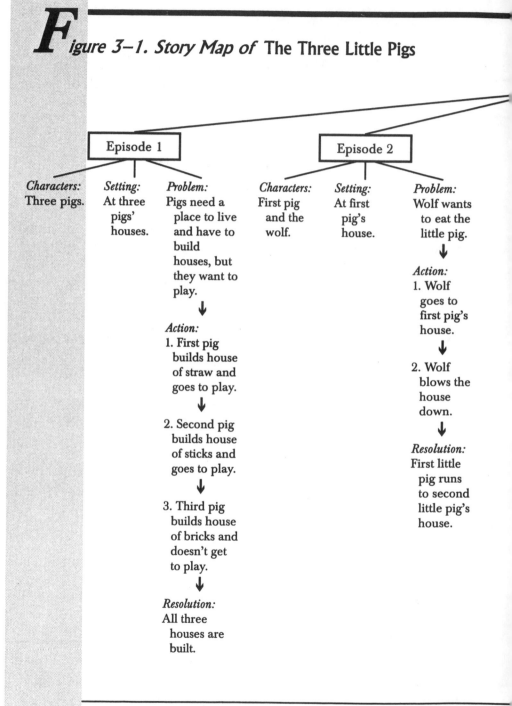

# *F*igure 3–1. *Story Map of* The Three Little Pigs

**Episode 1**

*Characters:*
Three pigs.

*Setting:*
At three
pigs'
houses.

*Problem:*
Pigs need a
place to live
and have to
build
houses, but
they want to
play.

↓

*Action:*
1. First pig
builds house
of straw and
goes to play.

↓

2. Second pig
builds house
of sticks and
goes to play.

↓

3. Third pig
builds house
of bricks and
doesn't get
to play.

↓

*Resolution:*
All three
houses are
built.

**Episode 2**

*Characters:*
First pig
and the
wolf.

*Setting:*
At first
pig's
house.

*Problem:*
Wolf wants
to eat the
little pig.

↓

*Action:*
1. Wolf
goes to
first pig's
house.

↓

2. Wolf
blows the
house
down.

↓

*Resolution:*
First little
pig runs
to second
little pig's
house.

*Source:* Cooper, J. David, *Literacy: Helping Children Construct Meaning,* Third Edition. Copyright © 1997 by Houghton Mifflin Company. Used with permission.

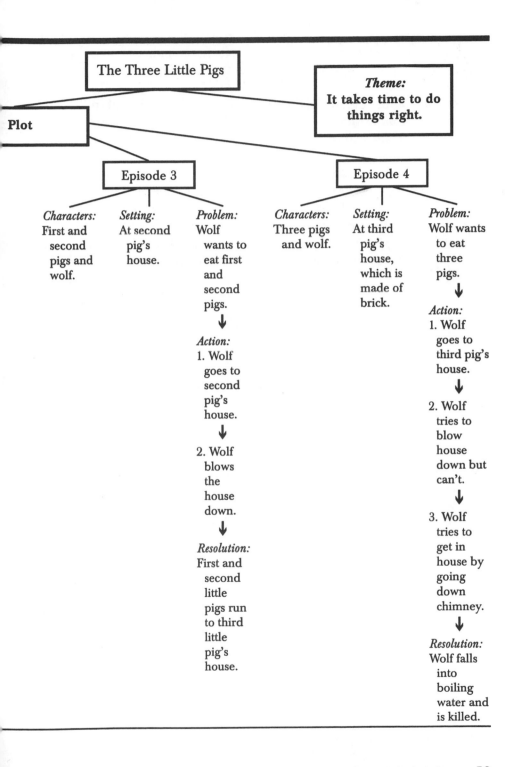

Every story has a plot and a theme, but the specific episodes making up the plot vary from story to story. Each episode has a setting, characters, and a problem to overcome. In complex stories the episodes become nested and intertwined.

*Expository texts* are organized differently than stories. Such texts might use descriptions, comparisons, cause-effect relationships, problem-posed/problem-solved formats, and so on. Table 3-1 provides a list of five kinds of expository text structures.

Familiarity with text structures aids comprehension because the listener/reader has an organizational scheme with which to think about what is being read. Text structure knowledge can be appreciated by considering our own knowledge of specific print contexts. Knowing how a road map is organized—knowing its structure—is essential in using it. If we didn't know how road maps were structured, we would have difficulty using one to find our way. The same is true of a restaurant menu. After having experience with menus, we know what to expect. There's a specific order to the listings, for example, and information about what is included in a dinner. Knowing the basic structure, we can more easily read other menus we encounter. It is the same with a cookbook, an instruction manual, a dictionary, a telephone book, or a book of songs.

The more exposure children have to narratives, the better they get at understanding how stories are organized. With each new story heard, comprehension becomes easier because the child's sense of story is increasing. When hearing expository text, children know that they must "change gears," that a different way of thinking is necessary because what they are hearing is not a story. Reading many types of books to children during the preschool and kindergarten years provides children with opportunities to learn how various kinds of texts are organized. (Various types of books—fiction, nonfiction, verse, and alphabet—are listed at the end of this chapter, on pp. 68–70.)

# Book reading and sensitivity to the sounds of language

In ordinary conversation, words are rarely juxtaposed in ways that cause us to compare one with another. But the language in books is often crafted so as to call our attention to the similarities and differences in the individual sounds in words. Sensitivity to small units of sound in the language is essential for learning to read and write an alphabetic script. Before considering specific examples of texts that have the power to focus our attention on the individual sounds of language, it is important to understand why this sensitivity is so critical to learning to read and write.

# *T*able 3–1. Examples of Expository Text Structures

| Expository Structure | Example |
|---|---|
| Description | The tiger is the master of the Indian jungle. It stalks its prey in deadly silence. For half an hour or more, it carefully watches and then slowly, placing one foot softly in front of the other, closes in. |
| Collection | As master of the Indian jungle, the male tiger plays many roles. First, he is the hunter of prey who stalks in deadly silence. He is the beauty of the jungle, an expert at doing nothing so that he can rest to be ready for his hunt. Finally, the lord of the jungle is the active seeker of mates, who begins his mating with a nuzzle but ends with a roar. |
| Causation or cause-effect | We observed the tiger from our vehicle as it stalked the herd of deer. As a result of the slight noise from our running camera, the tiger turned and knew we were there. This didn't stop it from returning to its intended prey. Slowly and carefully it moved forward, not making a sound. The deer were initially unaware of its presence, but because of the shifting winds they caught the tiger's scent. This was enough to scare them away. |
| Response, problem-solution, question-answer, or remark-reply | One problem to be resolved in tiger watching is transportation. How is it possible for observers to get close enough to a tiger without scaring it away or being attacked? Nature has helped solve this problem by making the tiger and the elephant friends. It is possible for an elephant carrying several people to get very near a tiger without even being noticed. If it weren't for this natural friendship, tiger watching would be virtually impossible. |
| Comparison | The power of the great tiger is like that of no other animal in the jungle. With one steady lunge, it can destroy its prey, *seemingly* without any effort at all. Unlike other predators, the tiger basks in the sun after an attack to prepare for its next kill. The actions of the tiger resemble those of no other animal in the Indian jungle. |

*Source:* Cooper, J. David, *Literacy: Helping Children Construct Meaning*, Third Edition. Copyright © 1997 by Houghton Mifflin Company. Used with permission.

## Phonemic segmentation and learning to read and write

In an alphabetic language, small units of sound—those smaller than a syllable—are coded with alphabet letters. These smallest units of sound are called *phonemes*. Each alphabet letter represents a phoneme. Some letters, such as *A, E,* and *C,* are used to represent more than one phoneme. It is also the case that specific letters are sometimes paired to represent a phoneme. For example, *ch* represents a phoneme, as does *th*.

A high level of phonemic awareness is demonstrated by a person's ability to segment a word into phonemes in temporal order, from the beginning of the word to its end. This is what someone does when sounding out a word in order to spell it. *Invented spellings,* children's first attempts to sound out and spell words, result in part because children cannot at first detect all of the phonemes in words and in part because children often code in nonconventional ways the phonemes they hear. For example, children might spell *cat* KT because they code the first phoneme with K rather than C and because they fail to detect the soft vowel phoneme in the middle of the word.

When we read words, rather than spell them, we start with the *graphemes* (that is, alphabet letters) and then translate these into phonemes. By putting these individual sounds together, we come up with an approximate pronounciation of an actual word. Knowing that we are trying to arrive at a word that makes sense in the context we are reading, we think about the exact word the approximation might sound like. Our oral vocabulary and background knowledge (see the discussion that follows) help us move quickly from a sound approximation to an accurate pronunciation of an actual word.

Until children have had experience thinking about words in terms of their sound components, or phonemes, such as when they say a word to themselves and segment each of its sounds before coding it with a letter (to spell it), they can be puzzled when moving from print to sound. A child might sound out the components of a printed word in a mechanical, stiff way and remain suspended at the sound approximation phase of decoding. The child is unable to come up with the word that is actually printed.

Poor oral vocabulary and weak background knowledge can contribute greatly to the problem of decoding printed words because few good candidates for words that make sense in the context are in the child's mind. However, an inability to think of oral language (words) as an ordered sequence of phonemes can also create this kind of problem (El Konin 1973). If unable to think about words in terms of a sequence of sounds, children are puzzled about what they are actually to do when decoding print.

It is not easy for children to become aware of language at the phoneme level. In ordinary conversation we process language at the individual sound level; otherwise we would not be able to know that someone is talking to us about *b*ats instead of *c*ats. (The difference of just one phoneme in these words results in entirely different meanings.) As we converse, however, we do not consciously think about language at this level. Instead, we concentrate on the meaning of what is being said.

To get at the meaning, we focus on individual words and on their context in sentences. We do not think very deliberately about even this because the process becomes quite automatic once we have learned to speak. But if we were to think about what occupies our mind when we are engaged in conversation, we would probably realize that we are thinking about the content of the message someone is trying to convey to us and about the meaning we want to convey in response. This requires our focusing on the meaning of words.

Conscious awareness of language at the phoneme level is learned (Liberman et al. 1974). It does not develop spontaneously with maturation, although some children might have more difficulty than other children with this aspect of language learning (Elbro, Borstrom, & Petersen 1998). Because awareness of language at this level is not naturally on our minds, specific experiences are necessary to help children begin to notice and think about this aspect of language. Early phoneme awareness consists of sensitivity to rhyme and alliteration. The ability to think about a word in terms of each of its phonemes, which is required when we sound out a word to spell it, comes much later.

It is this later *phonemic segmentation* ability that predicts so well a child's likelihood of success in beginning reading. Sensitivity to rhyme and alliteration is also related positively to later success in beginning reading (Bradley & Bryant 1983; Bryant et al. 1989), although it does not predict success in beginning reading nearly as strongly as does phonemic segmentation ability (Yopp 1988).

It is important, though, not to misinterpret this research. Sensitivity to rhyme and alliteration appear first (Goswami & Bryant 1992). Sensitivity to rhyme and alliteration might pave the way for the higher level of phonemic awareness required to segment words into their constituent phonemes. Without a beginning level of sensitivity to phonemes, which may be observed in children's detection of rhyme and alliteration, phonemic segmentation may be very slow in response to instruction.

### Using books to prime conscious sensitivity to phonemes

Children's first exposure to rhyme and alliteration might occur during early infancy when parents recite nursery rhymes or sing songs to provide entertainment or comfort. "Pat-a-Cake" is a favorite game of infants and toddlers. They love the clapping as the parent recites:

Pat-a cake, pat-a-cake, baker's man!
Bake me a cake as quick as you can.
Pat it and prick it and mark it with T,
And put it in the oven for Tommy and me.

Some rhymes come to a parent's or caregiver's mind at specific times. At bedtime or naptime, "Wee Willy Winkie" might be recited; during bathtime or handwashing, it might be "Rub-a-Dub, Dub, Three Men in a Tub." In the context of teaching a child how to treat a pet, an adult might recite "I Love Little Pussy."

Because many books for preschool and kindergarten children are written in verse, parents and teachers can keep language of this kind flowing into children's ears throughout the preschool and kindergarten years. This is not the only kind of language young children should hear, of course, but hearing a fair amount of it contributes to their sensitivity to sounds.

While reading books with rhyme and alliteration, teachers can comment, "Oh, 'duck' and 'stuck' rhyme," or "'sleepy' and 'slimy' sound the same at the beginning." Sometimes, when going back through a book in which rhyme and alliteration appear frequently, a teacher can review some of the rhyming words and ask, "What other words can you think of that rhyme with ____ and ____?" ("start like ___ and ___?").

Once children have been introduced to rhyme and alliteration word games ("What is another word that rhymes with ___?" "What is another word that begins like ___?"), they often initiate these games themselves, perhaps when having snack or lunch or when listening to a story in which they notice some rhyming words. (There is a list of predictable books at the end of Chapter 4; books made predictable through the use of rhyme are coded to indicate this.)

Teachers might also look for opportunities to talk with children about the sounds heard in the middle of words. In the song "Six Little Ducks," the words "wibble-wobble" sound alike at the beginning and at the end. The same is true of the words "creaky" and "croaky" in *One Duck Stuck*.

## Books and background knowledge

*Background knowledge* is the knowledge about the world we take with us to a book. As the poignant passage from Doris Kearns Goodwin's memoir illustrates, not only knowledge–information and facts–but also affect goes with us to a book.

The books I read filled my imagination, multiplying my daydreams, allowing me to supplement my own collection of stories, previously drawn mostly from my family and my neighbors, with characters and events far removed from the realities of Southard Avenue and Rockville Centre. . . . When I read about Little Toot's father, Big Toot, the fastest tugboat on the river, and his Grandfather Toot, who breathed smoke and told of mighty deeds, I pictured my uncle Willy and my grandfather Ephraim standing proudly at the helms of their ferryboats, navigating their ships expertly through the tricky currents of the waters surrounding New York and New Jersey. Because all my uncles and grandparents were dead, I had to find some way to keep them alive. By fusing what little I knew about their personalities into the characters I liked in the stories I read, I was able to surround myself with the large, vibrant family I always wished I had. And when Little Toot saved the stranded ocean liner and made his family proud, I imagined that someday I would do something that would bring me to the attention of my grandparents in heaven. (1997, 58–59)

Often certain characteristics of the characters in a book remind us of people we know or have heard about, and we can better relate to these characters, given our own experience with various people.

When a child says, "Hey, I have a pocket in my coat too," upon hearing that Peter in *The Snowy Day* is packing a snowball for his pocket, the child is bringing background knowledge to the book. Or when, in response to the same story, a child says, "The snowball won't stay a snowball in the house. Snow melts when it gets warm," the child is using background knowledge. A child who has experienced the unexpected disappearance of a snowball, because he did not understand at the time that snow melts when warmed, will probably feel an affinity for Peter, the main character in Keats's story. Similarly, a child who says, "Once I got stuck in some mud, and when my mom pulled my foot up, my boot came off," is also using her background knowledge. She is likely to understand very well the persistence of the duck seeking help to get out of the mud in *One Duck Stuck*.

A good storehouse of background knowledge is essential if children are to be good readers. It clearly helps children comprehend what they read (Pearson & Fielding 1991; Whitney et al. 1995). This knowledge also helps children decode words. Having attained sound approximations as the result of sounding out words, children can more quickly call to mind the printed words if they have an idea beforehand of which words would fit in this particular context. The process of reading is highly complex. Several different systems of knowledge and skill work together to support each other (Adams 1990). Background knowledge constitutes one important system.

For young children especially, real experience in the world is the primary source of background knowledge. Young children must see things, feel things, and try to do things if they are to gain the knowledge they need about the world. But books also help children develop background knowledge. Books provide opportunities for children to think about and thereby extend their own first-hand experiences.

Books also expose children to experiences they have not yet had. For example, a child may have played in the snow and even built a snowman, but the child may never have made angels in the snow, as Peter did in *The Snowy Day*. Through the child's own experience with snow, she may know that snow can cover the ground at a depth of several inches or more and that it will keep a pattern or shape when it is compressed or stepped in. Seeing Peter lying in the snow, moving his arms up and down, provides specific information to the child about how angels can be made. In this way, background information gained first from direct experience is broadened by books. In the process, the book itself contributes to the child's background knowledge.

If a program for young children is organized in terms of themes, units, or projects, teachers may obtain books (both informational/expository and narrative) to go along with the theme or unit. Whether children are studying plants, farm animals, insects, or color, many books can be found to accompany the unit of study. By coordinating firsthand experiences with the books made available to them, children gain knowledge, and this knowledge in turn aids their future reading of books. (See Schickedanz 1998 for an example of units in which direct-experience activities and books are included.)

## References

Adams, M. 1990. *Beginning to read: Thinking and learning about print.* Cambridge, MA: MIT Press.

Applebee, A.N. 1978. *The child's concept of story: Ages two to seventeen.* Chicago: University of Chicago Press.

Arnold, D.H., C.J. Lonigan, G.J. Whitehurst, & J.N. Epstein. 1994. Accelerating language development through picture book reading: Replication and extension to a videotape training format. *Journal of Educational Research* 86 (2): 235–43.

Beals, D.E., & P.O. Tabors. 1995. Arboretum, bureaucratic and carbohydrates: Preschoolers' exposure to rare vocabulary at home. *First Language* 15: 57–76.

Bradley, L., & P. Bryant. 1983. Categorizing sounds and learning to read—A causal connection. *Nature* 301 (3): 419–21.

Bryant, P.E., L. Bradley, M. Maclean, & J. Crossland. 1989. Nursery rhymes, phonological skills and reading. *Journal of Child Language* 16: 407–28.

Butler, S.R., H.W. Marsh, M.J. Sheppard, & L.J. Sheppard. 1985. Seven-year longitudinal study of the early prediction of reading acheivement. *Journal of Educational Psychology* 77: 349–61.

Chomsky, C. 1972. Stages in language development and reading exposure. *Harvard Educational Review* 42:1–33.

Crain-Thoreson, C., & P.S. Dale. 1992. Do early talkers become early readers? Linguistic precocity, preschool language, and emergent literacy. *Developmental Psychology* 28: 421–29.

Dickinson, D.K. 1984. First impressions: Children's knowledge of words gained from a single exposure. *Applied Psycholinguistics* 5: 359–73.

Dickinson, D.K., & M.W. Smith. 1994. Long-term effects of preschool teachers' book readings on low-income children's vocabulary and story comprehesion. *Reading Research Quarterly* 29 (2): 105–22.

Elbro, C., I. Borstrom, & D.K. Petersen. 1998. Predicting dyslexia from kindergarten: The importance of distinctness of phonological representations of lexical items. *Reading Research Quarterly* 33 (1): 36–60.

El Konin, D.B. 1973. Methods of teaching reading. In *Comparative reading*, ed. J. Downing, 551–78. New York: Macmillan.

Elley, W.B. 1989. Vocabulary acquisition from listening to stories. *Reading Research Quarterly* 24 (2):174-87.

Farrar, M.J. 1990. Discourse and the acquisitin of grammatical morphemes. *Journal of Child Language* 17: 607–24.

Goodwin, D.K. 1997. *Wait till next year: A memoir.* New York: Simon & Schuster.

Goswami, U., & P. Bryant. 1992. Rhyme, analogy, and children's reading. In *Reading acquisition*, eds. P.B. Gough, L.C. Ehri, & R. Treiman, 49–63. Hillsdale, NJ: Erlbaum.

Holdaway, D. 1979. *The foundations of literacy.* New York: Ashton Scholastic.

Liberman, I.Y., D. Shankweiler, F.W. Fischer, & B. Carter. 1974. Explicit syllable and phoneme segmentation in the young child. *Journal of Experimental Child Psychology* 18: 201–12.

Moerk, E.L. 1985. Picture book reading by mothers and young children and its impact upon language development. *Journal of Pragmatics* 9: 547–66.

Moerk, E.L. 1991. Positive evidence for negative evidence. *First Language* 11: 219–51.

Morgan, J.L., K.M. Bonamo, & L.L. Travis. 1995. Negative evidence on negative evidence. *Developmental Psychology* 31 (2): 180–97.

Nagy, W.E., R.C. Anderson, & P.A. Herman. 1987. Learning word meanings from context during normal reading. *American Educational Research Journal* 24: 237–70.

Pearson, P.D., & L. Fielding. 1991. Comprehension instruction. In *Handbook of reading research*, vol. 2, eds. R. Barr, M.L. Kamil, P.B. Mosenthal, & P.D. Pearson, 815–60. New York: Longman.

Pellegrini, A.D., J.C. Perlmutter, L. Galda, & G.H. Brophy. 1990. Joint book reading between Black Head Start children and their mothers. *Child Development* 61: 443-53.

Pikulski, J.J., & A.W. Tobin. 1989. Factors associated with long-term reading achievement of early readers. In *Cognitive and social perspectives for literacy research and instruction*, eds. S. McCormick, J. Zutell, P. Scharer, & P. O'Keefe. Chicago: National Reading Conference.

Ricard, R.J., & C.E. Snow. 1990. Language use in and out of context. *Journal of Applied Developmental Psychology* 11 (3): 251–66.

Robbins, C., & L.C. Ehri. 1994. Reading storybooks to kindergartners helps them learn new vocabulary words. *Journal of Educational Psychology* 86 (1): 54–64.

Schickedanz, J.A., & M. Sullivan. 1984. Mom, what does u-f-f spell? *Language Arts* 61 (1): 7–17.

Schickedanz, J.A., M.L. Pergontis, J. Kanosky, A. Blaney, & J. Ottinger. 1998. *Curriculum in early childhood.* Boston: Allyn & Bacon.

Senechal, M. 1997. The differential effect of storybook reading on preschoolers' acquisition of expressive and reflective vocabulary. *Journal of Child Language* 24 (1): 123–38.

Senechal, M., E. Thomas, & J. Monker. 1995. Individual differences in 4-year-old children's acquisition of vocabulary during storybook reading. *Journal of Educational Psychology* 87 (2): 218–29.

Snow, C. 1991. The theoretical basis for relationships between language and literacy in development. *Journal of Research in Childhood Education* 6 (1): 5–10.

Snyder, L.S., & D.M. Downey. 1991. The language-reading relationship in normal and reading-disabled children. *Journal of Speech and Hearing Research* 34: 129–40.

Stein, N.L. 1988. The development of children's storytelling skill. In *Child language*, eds. M.B. Franklin & S.S. Barten, 282–98. New York: Oxford University Press.

Sternberg, R., & W. Powell. 1983. Comprehending verbal comprehension. *American Psychologist* 38: 878–93.

Wells, G. 1985. *Language development in the preschool years.* Cambridge, UK: Cambridge University Press.

Whitehurst, G.J., F.L. Falco, C.J. Lonigan, J.E. Fischel, B.D. De Baryshe, M.C. Valdez-Menchoca, & M. Caulfield. 1988. Accelerating language development through picture book reading. *Developmental Psychology* 24 (4): 552–59.

Whitney, P., D. Budd, R.S. Bramucci, & R.S. Crane. 1995. On babies, bath water and schemata: A reconsideration of top-down processes in communication. *Discourse Processes* 20: 135–66.

Yopp, H.K. 1988. The validity and reliability of phonemic awareness tests. *Reading Research Quarterly* 23 (2): 159–77.

# Good books for preschoolers

There are dozens of excellent books for preschool children; the list provided here is by no means exhaustive. It is divided into four categories: fiction (narrative text/stories), nonfiction (expository text/information books), verse, and alphabet books.

## *Fiction (narrative text/stories)*

Asbjorsin, P. 1973. *The three billy goats gruff.* New York: Houghton Mifflin.

Asch, F. 1982. *Happy birthday moon.* Englewood Cliffs, NJ: Prentice-Hall.

Baby's First Golden Book Series. 1977. (Includes *Little animal friends, Winnie the Pooh's rhymes, What does baby see?* and *Play with me.*) Racine, WI: Western Publishing.

Barton, B. 1989. *Dinosaurs, dinosaurs.* New York: Crowell.

Brett, J. 1989. *The mitten.* New York: Putnam.

Carle, E. 1974. *The very hungry caterpillar.* New York: Philomel.

Carle, E. 1984. *The very busy spider.* New York: Philomel.

Carle, E. 1987. *A house for hermit crab.* New York: Simon & Schuster.

Carle, E. 1987. *The tiny seed.* New York: Scholastic.

dePaola, T. 1981. *Now one foot. Now the other.* New York: Putnam.

Dowell, P. 1991. *Zoo animals.* New York: Macmillan.

Ehlert, L. 1990. *Feathers for lunch.* Orlando, FL: Harcourt Brace Jovanovich.

Ehlert, L. 1990. *Fish eyes.* Orlando, FL: Harcourt Brace Jovanovich.

Ets, M. H. 1963. *Gilberto and the wind.* New York: Viking.

Freeman, D. 1968. *Corduroy.* New York: Viking.

Galdone, P., illustrator. 1968. *Henny Penny.* New York: Seabury.

Hoban, R. 1960. *Bedtime for Frances.* New York: Harper & Row.

Hutchins, P. 1974. *The wind blew.* New York: Macmillan.

Keats, E.J. 1962. *The snowy day.* New York: Puffin.

Keats, E.J. 1968. *A letter to Amy.* New York: Harper & Row.

Keats, E.J. 1979. *Over in the meadow.* New York: Parents Magazine Press.

Klinting, L. 1995. *Bruno the carpenter.* New York: Henry Holt.

Lionni, L. 1963. *Swimmy.* New York: Scholastic.

Lionni, L. 1986. *It's mine.* New York: Scholastic.

McCloskey, R. 1941. *Make way for ducklings.* New York: Penguin.

McCloskey, R. 1948. *Blueberries for Sal.* New York: Penguin.

Potter, B. 1902. *The tale of Peter Rabbit.* New York: Frederick Warne.

Root, P. (J. Chapman, illustrator). 1998. *One duck stuck.* Cambridge, MA: Candlewick.

Sendak, M. 1963. *Where the wild things are.* New York: Scholastic.

Seuss, Dr. 1957. *The cat in the hat.* New York: Random House.

Slobodkina, E. 1947. *Caps for sale.* Reading, MA: Addison-Wesley.

Viorst, J. 1977. *Alexander and the terrible, horrible, no good, very bad day.* New York: Atheneum.

Waddell, M. 1991. *Let's go home, Little Bear.* Cambridge, MA: Candlewick.

Walsh, E.S. 1989. *Mouse paint.* New York: Harcourt Brace Jovanovich.

## *Nonfiction (expository text/information books)*

*Baby's first book.* 1960. New York: Platt & Munk.

Back, C., & B. Watts. 1986. *Bean and plant.* New Jersey: Silver Burdett.

Barton, B. 1986. *Boats.* New York: Crowell.

Brenner, B., & B. Chardiet. (C. Schwartz, illustrator). 1993. *Where's that reptile?* New York: Scholastic.

Burnie, D. 1988. *Eyewitness books: Birds.* New York: Knopf.

de Bourgoing, P., & G. Jeunesse. 1991. *Fruit.* New York: Scholastic. (A First Discovery Book.)

Dowell, P. 1991. *Eye openers: Zoo animals.* New York: Aladdin.

Ehlert, L. 1989. *Planting a rainbow.* New York: Harcourt Brace Jovanovich.

Florian, D. 1991. *A potter.* New York: Greenwillow.

Florian, D. 1991. *Vegetable garden.* New York: Harcourt Brace Jovanovich.

Fujikawa, G. 1975. *Baby animals.* New York: Grosset & Dunlap.

Gibbons, G. 1985. *The milk makers.* New York: Aladdin.

Gibbons, G. 1987. *Trains.* New York: Scholastic.

Gibbons, G. 1988. *From seed to plant.* New York: Holiday.

Gillham, B. 1982. *The first words picture book.* New York: Coward, McCann, & Geogahan.

Heller, R. 1981. *Chickens aren't the only ones.* New York: Grosset & Dunlap.

Heller, R. 1982. *Animals born alive and well.* New York: Grosset and Dunlap.

Heller, R. 1995. *Color, color, color.* New York: Putnam & Grosset.

Jeunesse, G., & P. Biard. (P. Biard, illustrator). 1995. *Construction.* New York: Scholastic. (A First Discovery Book.)

Jeunesse, G., & P. de Bourgoing. 1989. *The egg.* New York: Scholastic. (A First Discovery Book.)

Jeunesse, G., & de Bourgoing, P. 1991. *The ladybug and other insects.* New York: Scholastic. (A First Discovery Book.)

Jeunesse, G., & Delafosse, C. 1992. *Musical instruments.* New York: Scholastic. (A First Discovery Book.)

Jeunesse, G., C. Delafoss, C. Millet, & D. Millet. (C. Millet & D. Millet, illustrators). 1990. *Castles.* New York: Scholastic. (A First Discovery Book.)

Jordan, H.J. (L. Krupinski, illustrator). 1992. *How a seed grows.* New York: HarperCollins.

Kredenser, G., & S. Mack. 1971. *One dancing drum.* New York: S.G. Phillips.

MacCarthy, P. 1989. *Animals galore!* New York: Dial.

Matchotka, H. 1991. *What neat feet!* New York: Morrow.

Mcmillan, B. 1988. *Growing colors.* New York: Mulberry.

Morris, A. (K. Heyman, photographer). 1989. *Hats, hats, hats.* New York: Scholastic.

Morris, A. 1993. *Bread, bread, bread.* New York: Morrow.

Morris, A. 1998. *Work.* New York: Morrow Junior Books.

Parsons, A. 1990. *Eyewitness juniors: Amazing mammals.* New York: Knopf.

Parsons, A. 1990. *Eyewitness juniors: Amazing snakes.* New York: Knopf.

Rockwell, A. 1984. *Trucks.* New York: Dutton.

Royston, A. 1992. *Eye openers: Baby animals.* New York: Aladdin.

Royston, A. 1992. *Eye openers: Insects and crawly creatures.* New York: Aladdin.

Shone, V. 1990. *Wheels.* New York: Scholastic.

## Verse

Aardema, V. 1981. *Bringing the rain to Kapiti Plain*. New York: Dial.

Ahlberg, A., & J. Ahlberg. 1978. *Each peach pear plum*. New York: Scholastic.

Carlstrom, N.W. (J.Pinkney, illustrator). 1987. *Wild, wild sunflower child Anna*. New York: Macmillan.

Hoberman, M.A. 1985. *A house is a house for me*. New York: Puffin.

Keats, E.J. (illustrator). 1971. *Over in the meadow*. New York: Scholastic.

Marzolla, J. 1995. *Sun song*. New York: HarperCollins.

Merriam, E. (D. Gottlieb, illustrator). 1992. *Train leaves the station*. New York: Henry Holt.

Prelutsky, J. (A. Lobel, illustrator). 1983. *Read-aloud rhymes for the very young*. New York: Knopf.

Serfozo, M. 1988. *Who said red?* New York: Scholastic.

Yolen, J. (L. Regan, illustrator). 1993. *Welcome to the green house*. New York: Putnam.

## Alphabet books

Ehlert, L. 1988. *Eating the alphabet*. New York: Harcourt Brace Jovanovich.

Geisel, T.S., & A.S. Geisel. 1963. *Dr. Seuss's ABC*. New York: Random House.

MacDonald, S. 1986. *Alphabetics*. New York: Scholastic.

Martin, B. 1989. *Chicka chicka boom boom*. New York: Simon & Schuster.

McPhail, D. 1989. *David McPhail's Animals A to Z*. New York: Scholastic.

Pallotta, J. (E. Stewart, illustrator). 1986. *The frog alphabet book*. Watertown, MA: Charlesbridge.

Pallotta, J., & B. Thompson. 1992. *The victory garden vegetable alphabet book*. Watertown, MA: Charlesbridge.

Pratt, K.I. 1992. *A walk in the rainforest*. Nevada City, CA: Dawn.

So, S. 1997. *C is for China*. Parisippany, NJ: Silver Press.

For all children the preschool years should be rich in opportunities to learn about reading and writing.

# Preschoolers and Books: Contexts for Reading, Props for Children's Play

In Chapter 3, we discussed how books provide a context in which children can learn about language and can deepen and extend their knowledge about the world. In this chapter, we discuss how children use books to practice reading and being a reader. We also discuss how books can be made available to children in a preschool classroom, both in a book center and as props to support children's play.

## Reading along with others, reading all by themselves

Children engage in two types of *practice reading* during their early years. The first is reading along with an adult. In this kind of practice, the adult scaffolds the child's reading of a book. In a *scaffolded* experience the child participates, but the adult does as much of the work as necessary to keep things going. Over time the adult does less and less of the task as the child takes over more and more.

The second type of practice is the *independent* retelling of a familiar story. In this kind of practice, a child reads a familiar storybook to herself, an adult, another child, or a doll or stuffed animal. Both reading along with adults and retelling stories independently are influenced by the opportunities children have to hear book language, learn about the structure of stories, learn about the world in general, and increase their knowledge about print and how it works.

As we discussed in Chapter 2, book babble is the first independent practice reading in which toddlers are likely to engage. A child opens and flips through a book while jabbering (using nonsense words). Book babble differs from conversational babble in that children sound as if they are reading rather than talking. The *prosody*—the rhythm of the speech—is like that of

Having seen and heard adults reading books aloud, many toddlers engage in book babble, producing nonsense sounds with the rhythm and pace of reading.

reading, not conversation. Although toddlers who have been read to capture in their book babble the unique sound features of someone reading, not a single word uttered is a real one. Toddlers are simply practicing the sound of reading; they are not trying to retell the actual words in a book.

The first attempt to retell what is actually in a book (the words in the book) usually occurs at about the same time a child begins to produce book babble or a little before. In these attempts, the child produces labels for pictures when he is looking through familiar books (that is, one-picture-to-a-page books). Usually, the picture-naming dialogue (a parent asks, "What's that?" and the parent or child answers with a name) is not reproduced in these independent practices. Instead, the child simply looks at the book and names the pictures he recognizes.

Once toddlers are introduced to books of verse or actual stories, they begin to chime in as the adult reads. They also begin to retell portions of familiar books when they are looking at them independently. Even though oral language is still quite limited, the child joins in. (See an example in "Language Development and Young Children's Practice Retellings" on pp. 74–75.) Predictable books are designed to make their texts memorable. (See pp. 77–78.) Their structure specifically encourages children to chime in as the adult reads and helps them recall chunks of text during independent retellings.

## Predictable books support chiming in and independent retelling

The structure of predictable books helps the adult elicit the child's participation. In Margaret Wise Brown's book *Goodnight Moon,* the narrative introduces key objects in a small bunny character's bedroom at bedtime. The rhyming built into the text and the clear and simple arrangement of text and illustrations help the child join in. For example, on a number of pages there are pairs of items having names that rhyme (kittens and mittens; clocks and socks). The adult can point to the pictures while reading the text. When he gets to the second word of the rhyming word pair, the reader can pause while pointing to the object in the picture. The picture, plus the cue from the rhyme, helps the child recall the needed word.

Later in the book, after each object in the room has been introduced, each is pictured again as the bunny tells it "goodnight." Here again, only one or two items appear on some pages. Moreover, the message is the same across the final pages as earlier: everything is named again as it is told "goodnight." Thus, portions of the text are quite easy to remember. As the adult reads, points, and pauses, a child who has heard the story only a few times can usually begin to join in on some of the pages.

# *L*anguage Development and Young Children's Practice Retellings

Very young children begin to retell parts of repetitive texts after they have had considerable experience in listening to them. A very young child's retellings will reflect the child's immature grammar and speech. This immaturity can be seen in the retellings of a favorite book by an 18-month-old boy. When hearing Dr. Seuss's *The Cat in the Hat,* he delighted in saying "Ish, No! No!" on the page that reads

**But our fish said, "No! No!**
**Make that cat go away!**
**Tell that Cat in the Hat**
**You do not want to play."**

He also liked to try to repeat the following lines from the same book: "Bump! Thump! Bump! Thump! / Down the wall in the hall."

The child became very excited in anticipating the four repetitions of "Sit!" found on the third page of the book.

Three characteristics of the boy's retellings are interesting. First, he elected to retell (or chime in on) passages that matched his own oral-language patterns. These included some holophrases and many two- to four-word sentences. The texts he liked most to repeat contained single words ("No! No!"; "Sit! Sit! Sit! Sit!"; "Bump! Thump!"), the use of which he had recently mastered.

Second, when he tried to repeat multiword utterances, he changed them to fit the level of the grammar in his own immature oral language. He did not say, "But our fish said, 'No! No!'" He said, "Ish, No! No!" Moreover, he said, "Down wall an hall" for "Down the wall in the hall."

Third, his articulation of words from the text was similar to his articulation in conversation. For example, he omitted the first phoneme in fish, pronouncing it "ish."

The constraints a child's grammar and articulation place on story retelling are less apparent with preschool children than with toddlers because preschoolers' language has progressed to more complex levels. But preschoolers often change irregular verbs to the past tense in accordance with the rules typically used with regular verbs. Thus, the word "felt" in a line from *The Very Hungry Caterpillar* is changed to "feeled" by many preschoolers when they retell the story.

Children who speak a dialect may translate standard English texts into their dialect during retellings. Preschool children who are learning English as a second language often retell a text using grammar that is typical of a second-language learner.

In all these cases, accuracy in retelling a story will increase over time not simply because the child has heard it many more times, but because his maturing oral language contains more of the standard language forms found in story texts.

There are other devices that make a text memorable. In *Barnyard Banter* by Denise Fleming, the same sentence frame is used throughout the book, words rhyme, and each animal's sound is repeated three times:

Mice in the grain bin, squeak, squeak, squeak.

Peacocks in the wire pen, shriek, shriek, shriek.

Donkeys in the paddock, hee, haw, haw.

Crows in the cornfield, caw, caw, caw.

Crickets in the stone wall, chirp, chirp, chirp.

Frogs in the pond, blurp, blurp, blurp.

Children soon notice both the basic rhythm of the repeating sentence and the repetitions of the animal sounds. They begin to chime in on the second or third repetition of an animal sound after hearing the adult read the first.

The animals themselves are easy to recognize in the big, bold illustration across each two-page spread. This recognition prompts the child's recall of the first word of text on each page. The context in which an animal might be found (grain bin, wire pen, cornfield, stone wall, pond) is included in the illustration. If the child has background knowledge about these things, it helps her recall these words.

Finally, in animal pairs, the sounds produced by the first animal rhyme with the sounds produced by the next. The child's knowledge of animal sounds, coupled with support provided by rhyme, helps prompt recall of these parts. The adult holds everything together by scaffolding the reading—by doing the basic reading while providing slots for the child to chime in. The reader's pointing to pictures, pausing, and holding on longer to the beginning sound of a word all help the child participate.

After a child has participated a number of times in a scaffolded reading experience with a particular book, she usually attempts to retell the story independently. Of course, children go back and forth between scaffolded and independent readings of a book, often over a period of many months. Usually, at some point the child has memorized the full text of a highly predictable book and can retell it perfectly.

A short description of the structural devices a book employs to make a text memorable and a list of predictable books can be found in the box on pages 77 to 78. Each book is coded to indicate the specific devices used. The list is not exhaustive, but it includes many good examples of predictable books.

# *P*redictable Books: A Bibliography

Various literary devices make books predictable. These include (1) rhyming; (2) repetition of a basic sentence frame with only one or two words varied each time; (3) use of a refrain; (4) cumulative text (one new sentence is added on each page, and text introduced previously is repeated on each successive page); (5) a close relationship between illustrations and text (every item or action mentioned in the text is pictured); and (6) placing on each page text covering only one idea or thought. Each book listed below is coded with numbers indicating which devices it uses.

Bang, M. 1983. *Ten, nine, eight.* New York: Scholastic. (1, 5, 6)

Barton, B. 1991. *The three bears.* New York: HarperCollins. (2, 3, 5)

Brown, M.W. 1947. *Goodnight moon.* New York: Harper & Row. (1, 2, 5, 6)

Burningham, J. 1975. *The blanket.* New York: Crowell. (1, 5, 6)

Carle, E. 1969. *The very hungry caterpillar.* New York: Philomel. (2, 5, 6)

Carle, E. 1984. *The very busy spider.* New York: Philomel. (2, 5)

Cowley, J., & J. Melser. 1980. *Mrs. Wishy-Washy.* Auckland, New Zealand: Shortland Publications, Ltd. (2, 3, 5, 6)

Degan, B. 1983. *Jamberry.* New York: HarperCollins. (1, 2, 5)

Flack, M. 1932. *Ask Mr. Bear.* New York: Macmillan. (2, 5, 6)

Fleming, D. 1993. *In the small, small pond.* New York: Henry Holt. (1, 2, 5, 6)

Fleming, D. 1994. *Barnyard banter.* New York: Scholastic. (1, 2, 5, 6)

Florian, D. 1991. *Vegetable garden.* New York: Harcourt Brace Jovanovich. (1, 5, 6)

Fox, M. (illus. P. Mullins). 1986. *Hattie and the fox.* New York: Aladdin. (3,4, 5, 6)

Fox, M. (illus. C. Whitman). 1996. *Zoo-looking.* New York: Scholastic. (1, 2, 5)

Galdone, P. 1968. *Henny Penny.* New York: Scholastic. (2, 3, 4, 5)

Galdone, P. 1973. *The little red hen.* New York: Scholastic. (2, 5)

Heller, R. 1981. *Chickens aren't the only ones.* New York: Grosset & Dunlap. (1, 3, 5)

Hoberman, M.A. (illus. B. Fraser). 1982. *A house is a house for me.* New York: Puffin Books. (1, 2, 3, 5)

Hudson, C., & B.C. Ford. (illust. G. Ford). 1990. *Bright eyes, brown skin.* New York: Scholastic. (1, 5, 6)

Hutchins, P. 1974. *The wind blew.* New York: Macmillan. (1, 5, 6)

*(continued on p. 78)*

*(Predictable Books continued)*

Hutchins, P. 1968. *Rosie's walk*. New York: Macmillan. (5, 6)

Kalan, R. (illus. N.W. Parker). 1981. *Jump, frog, jump!* New York: Scholastic. (3, 4, 5)

Keats, E.J. 1971. *Over in the meadow*. New York: Scholastic. (1, 2, 5)

Lewison, W.C. (illus. H. Wilhelm). 1992. *Buzzzz said the bee*. New York: Scholastic. (1, 2, 5, 6)

Martin, B. 1970. *Brown bear, brown bear*. New York: Holt, Rinehart & Winston. (2, 5, 6)

Martin, B., & J. Archambault. (illus. T. Rand). 1987. *Here are my hands*. New York: Henry Holt. (1, 2, 5, 6)

Mirriam, E. (illus. D. Gottlieb). 1992. *Train leaves the station*. New York: Henry Holt. (1, 5)

Neitzel, S. (illus. N.W. Parker.) 1989. *The jacket I wear in the snow*. New York: Greenwillow. (2, 4, 5)

Neitzel, S. (illus. N.W. Parker). 1997. *The house I'll build for the wrens*. New York: Greenwillow. (2, 4, 5)

Peppe, R. 1970. *The house that Jack built*. New York: Delacorte. (2, 4, 5)

Raffi. (illus. N.B. Westcott). 1987. *Down by the bay*. New York: Crown. (1, 2, 3, 5)

Root, P. (illus. J. Chapman). 1998. *One duck stuck*. Cambridge, MA: Candlewick. (1, 2, 3, 5, 6)

Slobodkina, E. 1940, 1947. *Caps for sale*. New York: Harper Trophy. (3, 5)

Trapani, I. 1993. *The itsy bitsy spider*. New York: Scholastic. (1, 5, 6)

Winthrop, E. (illus. W. Joyce). 1986. *Shoes*. New York: Harper & Row. (1, 2, 5)

Wood, A. 1992. *Silly Sally*. New York: Scholastic. (1, 2, 3, 5)

# Strategies used in storybook reading

Researchers who have studied children's retellings of their familiar and favorite storybooks have found some general trends in children's behavior. In the early 1980s Elizabeth Sulzby conducted an extensive study of young children's story-reading behavior (Sulzby 1985). Children ranging in age from 2 to 6 years were asked to read familiar storybooks, including two of their own favorites.

Sulzby found that children's behaviors differed across age groups. Some ways of reading were more characteristic of the younger children, while other ways were more characteristic of the older children. The following trends were found:

**1.** Younger children tend to treat each page of a book as a separate unit, not as part of an overall story (categorized as *story not formed*). Older children, on the other hand, tend to respond to each page as if it is part of an overall story (*story formed*) (Sulzby 1985, 464).

**2.** The language younger children use tends to resemble oral language more than written language. That is, younger children sound like they are *telling* a story rather than reading it. But when older children read a familiar book, they sound more like they are actually reading the story, not telling it.

**3.** Readings by younger children tend to be guided by the pictures. As children get older, the print begins in various ways to guide the child's reading.

From these trends we can see that over a period of years fairly gradual changes take place in a child's way of reading. For example, children change from retelling stories in their own words (paraphrasing the text) to reciting them verbatim. With regard to using print rather than pictures to guide the reading, there is movement from never actually looking at the print—even being unaware of its existence—to swiping a hand over the print even though the pictures are prompting the child's recall of the text appearing on the page. Over time, children still use pictures as clues to recall text, but they know that what they are saying is specified by the print on the page. They swipe at the print to appear more like the adult readers they have observed. Children who know that the print tells the story and that the print is read by the adult story reader are likely also to be more careful handling the book than are children who do not yet know: they avoid covering the print with their hands while holding a book for an adult to read.

Similarly, children who are aware that print tells the story are not disconcerted when the adult, coming to a textless page (such as those in *Where the Wild Things Are*), chats about the pictures. By contrast, younger children are likely to protest when the adult chats about the pictures on textless pages. Unaware of print and its function, they expect the reading to go on and are

> Until adults start reading children stories, children have little opportunity to learn about the more formal structures used in written language.

not satisfied with mere discussion. They notice and protest when the adult uses language that is more characteristic of oral language than book language. They want the adult to *read* the story, that is, talk in book language, not just to talk about it. Children who understand that print tells the story in a book will notice when there is no print on the pages. These children do not protest the shift in the adult's language because they understand that there is no print to read on these pages.

A key question about any age-related changes in children's behavior is, What causes a child to progress from beginning levels to more advanced levels? In this case the question is, What, if anything, can be done to help a child progress in story-reading behavior?

### Storybook-reading behavior: Experience matters

Sulzby (1985) cautions the reader against thinking of the trends she observed in storybook reading as stages because this word implies maturationist theory. *Stages* are specific epochs or periods of development, each marked by unique characteristics, determined by maturational changes. A stage conception of development does *not* explain very well the progress children make in reading their storybooks. The trends or patterns Sulzby observed are age related, to be sure, but age trends are as much the result of the sequence in which children are provided various experiences as they are the result of movements forward in maturation.

Of course, adults select particular books to read to very young children because they feel that these books are the ones very young children can best understand. As is the case in many areas of development, child characteristics at a particular point in time cause us to provide one kind of experience rather than another.

This sort of interaction between maturation and experience, which is found throughout childhood, makes it virtually impossible to sort out the independent effects of maturation and experience. Thus it is futile to speak of maturation *versus* experience. Both fuel changes in children. The important point here is to know that maturation alone does not lead to changes in children's story reading. Of course, maturation limits what is possible at any particular point in time, but without experience the child will progress little, if at all, in story-reading behavior.

We saw in Chapter 3 that experience with books can affect a child's language development in many ways and that experience with books can expand a child's background knowledge. In our discussion here we explore how experience with books is likely to affect children's practice reading of familiar books.

**From "story not formed" to "story formed," and from "oral-language-like" to "written-language-like."** The first books parents read to children are rarely stories. Instead, they are books of pictures, usually without any text, except for labels. These books elicit naming behavior, not storytelling behavior, from the parent.

The next books shared with children are likely to be theme books (scenes from the bedtime or bathtime routine, for example), not storybooks. Theme books show a sequence of related events. These books elicit more than labels from the parent, but the "and then" talk elicited is still not a story. For example, in Gyo Fujikawa's *Sleepytime,* sleepy children are shown getting ready for bed and then asleep in bed:

First, there's bathtime...
or a shower...
to get clean.
Don't forget to brush teeth!
Then hop into bed,
turn out the light, and "Good night!"

In plotted narratives, the causal links between and among events are psychological; that is, they hinge on the desires and motives of the characters. These psychologically based, causal connections give stories their cohesiveness. Theme books do not call for this kind of cohesive linking of the events they depict. Rather, there is a "first this, then that, and then that" structure without an underlying "because" of the kind we find in actual stories.

Object-naming and theme books also elicit talking by the adult and child throughout the reading, such as when a picture is described and related to an object a child owns or sees frequently. Later, when actual stories are read, large portions of the book—even the whole book—are read without back-and-forth discussion. Talking about the story usually takes place *after* the book has been read through once, perhaps as the adult and child go through the book a second time. Until adults start reading stories to children, children have little opportunity to learn about the more formal structures used in written language. Among other things, these more formal written-language structures are *monologic* (one person—the narrator of the story—talks for a long time) rather than *dialogic* (at least two people talk back and forth, as in conversation) (Sulzby 1985).

Thus, the trends in story-reading behavior, from story not formed to story formed and from oral-language-like to written-language-like, reflect in part the order in which experience in hearing actual stories is acquired. Younger children talk about books in the ways they have heard books talked about: they label pictures or describe (tell about) each page, treating it as an isolated event. As they hear more actual stories, their talk becomes more like written language, and each page is treated as part of an overall story.

Variations in the age at which individual children begin to form stories when retelling books might also be related to oral-language experience *outside* the book-reading context. Experience in constructing personal or autobiographical narratives might affect a child's ability to form stories in retelling books.

We discussed in Chapter 2 how many parents begin to talk with children about recent shared experiences when children are about 18 months of age. (See p. 25.) Studies of parents' scaffolding of children's recall or reconstruction of these shared experiences show that parents vary widely in skill. Some parents seem to know how to alter their questions to provide the cues or information needed by a child to recall part of a shared event. Other parents repeat the question rather than provide new information that might prompt the child's recall.

These and other variations in parental scaffolding style and skill are related to children's subsequent skill in producing well-formed personal narratives (Peterson & McCabe 1992, 1994). These early variations in the oral-language/personal-narrative domain could affect children's skill in retelling fictional narratives they have heard in books.

**From picture-governed to print-governed reading.** As we discussed earlier, picture books use illustrations to aid children's comprehension of the text. At first, parents utilize the illustrations as they read by pointing to pictures and talking about them. Later they point more to the print, indicating to the child that the print tells them exactly what to say. Seeing adults point to the print as they read helps children understand that the print, not the pictures, actually tells the story in a book.

Toddlers and young preschoolers sometimes ask questions about print, especially if it is embedded in the illustrations where it is likely to catch their attention. Many picture books are designed so that the illustrations cover a two-page spread. When looking at the illustrations, the child often notices the print. Picture books in which print is placed on the illustrations use large, bold type not arranged in standard lines. *Barnyard Banter* is an example of a book in which large, bold text is drawn practically right on top of the illlustrations. *In the Small, Small Pond* and *In the Tall, Tall Grass* by Denise

Fleming and *Feathers for Lunch* by Lois Ehlert are other examples of books designed in this way.

The transition from picture-governed to print-governed retellings is an especially interesting and important one. Because many researchers (for example, Durkin 1966; Clark 1976) have found that virtually all early readers seem to have been launched down the road toward conventional reading by first *fingerpoint reading* (that is, pointing to the word as they recite it) their favorite storybooks, many early educators have concluded that listening to predictable books and then practicing reading them independently or with an adult is about all that it takes to help children learn to read. But simply seeing adults point to print or simply asking adults what the big, bold words above the illustrations say is not all that is required for children's readings to become guided by print. Children must have some specifically print-related knowledge (Ehri & Sweet 1991); otherwise, they continue to use picture-guided reading strategies indefinitely.

Children begin using print to guide their retelling of familiar books when they have acquired some basic knowledge about print, such as the sounds of initial letters.

First, children must know alphabet letters by name. Second, children must know how to segment a spoken word into its constituent phonemes, in sequence. Finally, children must have the idea that alphabet letters are associated systematically with specific sounds or phonemes. With this information and skill under their belts, children can fingerpoint read.

Pictures prompt children's recall of the text appearing on a specific page, just as they prompt recall in all types of emergent reading. But when children fingerpoint read, they think about each word just before they recite it. A child isolates the first sound of the next word recalled from the text. Then the child must think about the alphabet letter used to represent it. This letter's visual configuration then comes to mind, and the child searches to find a printed word that begins with that letter. As she locates this word on the page, the child points to it just as she recites it.

Phonemic awareness and segmentation ability can be taught in several ways. We explained in Chapter 3 how experience with books containing rhyme and alliteration helps children become aware of language at the phoneme level. (See pp. 64–65.) One of the best ways to help children develop skill in phonemic segmentation is to sound out words (that is, isolate phonemes in sequence) when children ask for spellings of words. (See Chapter 5,"Preschoolers and Writing," for information about providing demonstrations of phonemic segmentation.)

Children can also be helped to distinguish among, and learn the names of, alphabet letters in a number of ways. (In Chapter 6 the section titled "Teaching about theAlphabet in Authentic Contexts," pp. 146–147, offers specific suggestions.)

Letter-sound associations need not be taught specifically, one at a time. Children are able to use their knowledge of letter names to associate letters with sounds/phonemes. Saying a letter name, one hears in most cases the phoneme that letter represents. To begin to link letters and sounds, all a child needs is the basic idea of letter-sound associations–the knowledge that letters are selected systematically to represent sounds. Demonstrations of systematic linking, such as those provided when adults spell words children request, help children get this basic idea. (Again, see Chapter 5.)

Because fingerpoint reading is done within the context of a very familiar book rather than an unfamiliar book, it is still a form of emergent reading. The child works from a memorized, oral version of a very familiar text.

We say someone is reading when she is able to decode print in an unfamiliar book. Among reading scholars, this is called *conventional reading*. A *beginning reader* is one who reads conventionally but is still a novice. Beginning readers misread quite a few words, and they typically revise the first reading of a word when they realize that it does not make sense given its context. Children gradually get better at using and coordinating several kinds

> Children gradually get better at using and coordinating various kinds of information that enable them to get meaning from print.

of information: *graphophonemic* information (letter and sound relationships), *morphophonemic* information (how to pronounce letter sequences found in common prefixes and suffixes), and *background knowledge and language* information (information about context). Children become increasingly adept at using these cues, and they continue for years and years to improve their reading. We say that *learning* to read has been achieved once a child has managed to coordinate all of these cueing systems in a fairly smooth way.

## *Reluctance to read: Preludes to a major step forward*

Sometimes children are reluctant to "read" a story independently when requested. A child's willingness may depend on his current understanding of what reading a story means as well as on his judgment of his ability to read a particular story in a way that is consistent with this understanding.

For example, in a study of preschoolers' story-reading behavior, children without much book experience were often willing to create a story for an unfamiliar book by looking at the book's illustrations and making up a story (Rossman 1980). Children who were somewhat more experienced with books, however, would not make up a story, although they were willing to tell in their own words the story they knew was in the book. Children even more experienced told the story exactly and asked about the words they could not recall. When asked to read a completely unfamiliar book, they often refused to retell it, saying, "I don't know the words in that one; you read it" (Rossman 1980).

Sometimes adults view with some dismay a child's reluctance to try to read a book, especially if the child has been willing to retell the book on many previous occasions. However, the child's unwillingness may indicate an increase in the child's understanding about the exactness and stability of stories when they are printed in books. In this case, reluctance indicates progress rather than a problem.

Often the child who refuses to retell a story will insist that the adult read the book. It is important that the adult respond to such requests as much as possible because the adult's demonstration of reading the book provides the child with more information about the particular story, about the specific *words* used to tell the story, and about where in the book specific *words are located*. The child's current level of understanding about books usually dictates the specific information the child focuses on and picks up. In time—often in a matter of a few weeks—the child is likely to use information gained from these observations of adult reading to achieve a new level of independent story retelling.

## Learning to enjoy reading and being a reader

A major contribution of story-reading experience is the pleasure that it can bring. First of all, stories are often very interesting. They tell of other children, animals, funny situations, and frightening events that typically turn out all right. To enter into the world of stories on their own is something that many children want to do once they have experienced the joy that stories can bring. Thus, experience with stories can build a positive attitude toward reading and can develop a strong desire to learn to read.

In addition to the interest in the stories themselves, there is an emotional component of the story-reading experience in the positive, personal interaction between adult and child. Story reading often takes place with the child on the parent's or caregiver's lap or snuggled side by side. The bedtime story may be one of the most positive times of the day for parent and child, especially if it is a nightly ritual. Because the adult and child know the routine, the negotiation that characterizes other activities during the day is not present. The book, as the basis for interaction, makes talking together easy. The prospect of soon having a few hours without the many necessary interruptions that come with caring for young children may make parents particularly calm and nurturant during story-reading time. Story reading is also often wrapped up with the bedtime rituals of the goodnight kiss and the tucking in, which are among the most nurturing and positive of parent-child interactions.

In *Family Literacy,* Taylor suggests that "the seemingly benign literate activity of reading bedtime stories to the preschool child can permeate years of family life" (1983, 83). It probably permeates years of school life too. If experience with books is enjoyable, and if it occurs under especially nurturant conditions, the feelings associated with reading and books are likely to be highly positive. The development of such positive attitudes toward books and reading is one of the most important contributions of early book-reading experiences.

# Making books available to children in the preschool classroom

We have seen in this chapter and the previous one how extremely important the story-reading experience is to children's literacy development. Perhaps no other activity contributes so much. How, then, can we support story reading and exploration of books in group programs for young children? What can we do to ensure that children have access to good books and stories?

The recommendations about making children's books accessible are based on four assumptions:

1. the room is organized into learning centers;

2. a collection of books is kept in a special book area in the room, and books and other print materials also are placed in other areas to support children's play and engagement in projects and activities;

3. the daily schedule includes an extended period for children to choose among activities; and

4. the daily schedule includes a story time.

## *Selecting books for and displaying books in a book area*

Making books available in the classroom may not be enough to draw children to them. How books are displayed can make a big difference in thier use; which books are offered also influences children's interest in the books provided.

**Type of books.** Books offered to young children in the book area should be good-quality children's literature; some should have highly predictable texts. (See "Predictable Books: A Bibliography," pp. 77–78.) In a book area it is wise to include some familiar books, a couple of relatively new ones, a few that are very simple, and some that are more complex. The books should represent a variety of topics to accommodate a range of interests. It is also nice to include in the book area books made by the children and perhaps a photo album of school events with captions explaining what each photo depicts.

Books placed in other areas of the room, to support nature study or block building, are often information books rather than storybooks. For example, books showing pictures of castles or how a house is built, from start to finish, can be placed on shelves in the block area to inspire children's building. Good examples of books suitable for this context are Byron Barton's

*Building a House,* Gail Gibbons's *How to Build a House,* and the First Discovery Book *Castles.*

Nature study can be supported by placing a book or two near a display. The Eyewitness Book *Seashells* can be included with a collection of seashells. If chicken eggs are incubating, the First Discovery Book *Eggs* and the See How They Grow Book *Duck* could be placed nearby. If a snakeskin is displayed, the Eyewitness Junior Book *Amazing Snakes* could be provided. Adults can point out features in the book relevant to what the children can see in the actual specimens.

**Appeal of the book-area display.** The way books are displayed influences the book area's attractiveness and children's interest in spending time in this part of the room. Teachers might want to stand back and take a good look at the book area. Does the book display look interesting? Colorful? Uncluttered? Can a child who enters the area find a specific book without having to search? Are book covers visible? If the display rack does not hold books so as to show their covers, teachers can stand up a limited number of books.

The physical and emotional comfort of the book area is also important. Is there a child-size rocking chair in the area? Are there pillows? Is the area carpeted? Is the area small and cozy, or is it so large that it does not appear to be a protected, special place? Rawson and Goetz (1983) report that a small, cozy book center attracts children more than a larger one does. Of course, if an area is too small, children will not be comfortable and the out-loud retelling of a story by one child might disturb the book browsing of another.

**Listening post, flannel boards, and puppets.** A tape recorder with jacks for headphones can provide story-listening opportunities to children during activity time. The listening area can be part of the book area or adjacent to it. Even three or four books with tapes add considerably to the classroom. To make more durable the paperback books that come with tapes, teachers can cover them with clear contact paper. Children can use the tape recorder independently once the teacher has given a demonstration during group story time. Although machines are no substitute for the interactive reading an adult can provide, a listening post can extend the story-listening opportunities available to children during busy times of the day.

Flannel-board pieces and puppets relating to familiar stories can also be available in a book area. As Morrow (1993) notes, stories most suited to flannel-board presentation have a limited number of characters because this limits the number of pieces needed to reenact the story. If too many flannel-board pieces are required to tell a story, it becomes difficult to manage them. If teachers wish to make flannel-board materials for books requiring many pieces, it is wise to connect several items to a background piece of felt. For

Children spend more time interacting with books when the classroom has a comfortable, attractive book area.

example, for *The Very Hungry Caterpillar,* all the pieces of each kind of fruit (plums, pears, oranges, strawberries) can be mounted on one piece of felt instead of being provided as individual pieces. Or all the fruit can be mounted in rows on one piece of felt, and a small caterpillar can be provided for a child to move over each row as the caterpillar in the story eats through it. The felt pieces for the junk-food pages can be presented in the same manner, with five or six food items per piece of felt. By attaching felt pieces together, the teacher reduces considerably the likelihood that they will become scattered. This kind of organization also helps children recall chunks of the story.

Puppets work best for stories with dialogue (Morrow 1993). There are many ways to design puppets, of course, but stick puppets can work best in a book area where one child might sometimes be the sole puppeteer. Using hand puppets can interrupt the flow of the story because it takes time to put them on and take them off. Stick puppets, however, can be picked up and put down quickly, making it possible for children to move the story along.

> Children enjoy and benefit from being read to in small groups and individually in addition to joining in group storytime.

Both flannel-board materials and puppets should first be introduced by a teacher, perhaps during a group storytime. The teacher's use of them will demonstrate to children how they work.

Teachers must also work out how to make the materials available to children. Flannel-board pieces can be kept on a cafeteria-style tray. Because a tray provides a fairly large surface, it is possible to spread pieces out, thus making them easier to find when needed.

Stick puppets can also be kept on a tray. A large piece of tagboard can be used to line the tray, and individual sections can be drawn on the tagboard with a marker. In each section a smaller picture of a stick puppet can be drawn, and the stick puppets can then be arranged on the tagboard, each in its own section. Organization like this helps children find a puppet when they need it. It also helps children arrange the puppets when they are finished with them, making them readily available for another child.

**Care of books.** Keeping books organized in the book area and providing appropriate storage space help children to take care of books. When books are crammed into cartons or boxes, children must remove many to locate the one they want. The books removed often remain on the floor and are stepped on. If good display and storage furniture is in short supply, it would be better to provide fewer books in a classroom collection at any one time and then rotate them fairly often.

The books included in a book area, in the block area, or alongside nature-study displays should always be complete and well cared for. When pages are torn, teachers can help children mend them with tape. If a book has been used so much that its pages are coming out of its binding, the pages can sometimes be removed, individually laminated, and then held together in a metal-ring binder. Books completely worn out should be discarded.

### Providing social support for children's use of books

Although the physical characteristics of the book corner and other areas where books are used are instrumental in inviting children to read, they alone are not enough. Teachers must support the use of books in the classroom with their presence. Otherwise some children may not use books at all or may use them in ways that are not particularly productive.

Often teachers never enter the book area during the daily choice or activity time. Rather, they tend to supervise art or cooking projects or get materials ready for an activity scheduled for later in the day. Or because the book center is not an area where safety or extreme messiness are issues, teachers may ignore it during activity time. Teachers also may think it unnecessary for them to visit the book area because they read to children daily during the scheduled group story time.

Children, however, benefit from being close to the book when it is read, from having their favorite stories reread many times, and from having their individual questions answered. Children also benefit when teachers look at books with them as part of an ongoing nature study or other focused investigation.

Teachers need not spend a great deal of time in the book area to have an effect. In one study, children chose to go to the book corner most often when teachers were there intermittently, not when they were never there, nor when they were there all the time (Rawson & Goetz 1983). In other words, children spent the most time in the book corner during activity time when a teacher was there once in a while. Perhaps when teachers are never in the book area, children who need the close emotional support of an adult to explore an area will not venture in. Another factor may be children's desire to interact with teachers. Children often go where a teacher is simply to talk to the teacher. But after arriving in the area, the child may notice what is going on and become interested or may be invited by the teacher to join in. As a result, more children are likely to be exposed to the book area if teachers sometimes spend time there.

Total teacher absence from the book corner may deter children from going there. This in turn can decrease children's opportunities for individual scaffolded-reading practice. If teachers rarely read books or read them only during large group story time, children may not receive the individual scaffolded experience they need to launch independent retellings of favorite books.

Constant teacher presence, on the other hand, might diminish visits to a book corner, especially if it is a small, cozy, comfortable place for children to go when they wish to be by themselves. If adults are always present, children are likely to seek other places to enjoy some privacy. Some children may prefer to practice-read out of adult earshot.

Being present in the book area on an intermittent basis seems to be the best practice in most cases. Teachers might consider briefly visiting the book center a few times in each daily activity period, or they may choose to visit for somewhat longer periods several times a week, as the schedule allows. This a good place to ask classroom volunteers to help out. Seniors or high- school volunteers, who join an all-day program after they finish their own school day, are a tremendous help. As children's energy lags late in the day, the book corner becomes an especially attractive area for them to visit.

# *L*iteracy Props for Dramatic Play

## House play

Trade books to read to dolls or stuffed animals (include some small books designed for infants)

Telephone books (telephone numbers, children's names, addresses; cover pages with clear plastic adhesive)

Cookbooks (mount classroom cooking recipes on tagboard, laminate, place in three-ring binders)

Empty food, toiletry, and cleaning containers

Emergency numbers decal to attach to the play phone (phone numbers for doctor, ambulance, fire station, and police)

Small notepads and a container with pencils

Wall plaques with appropriate verses

Stationery and envelopes

Magazines and newspapers

Food coupons

Grocery store food ads

Play money

## Doctor's office play

Trade books for waiting room (include small ones, designed for children to read to sick babies)

Magazines for the waiting room

Telephone book for receptionist's desk

Eye chart posted on the wall (make one with rows of different-size letters)

Message pad and pencils

Signs such as Doctor Is In, Doctor Is Out, No Smoking, Open, and Closed

Pamphlets for children about health care (brushing teeth, eating good foods, wearing seat belts)

File folders and ditto sheets for health charts

Index cards (cut in quarters) for appointment cards

## Grocery store play

Empty food containers

Labels for store departments: Dairy, Produce, Bakery, and so on

Food posters (ask a supermarket for old ones)

Brown paper bags with the name of the store written on them

# Books as props to support children's play

Aaron sits in the waiting room of the classroom doctor's office. The doctor is busy with a patient. Aaron bides his time, reading a children's book he found in the waiting room.

Jessica is also visiting the doctor's office. She holds her doll, who is sick. She reads quietly to her from a small book she found in a basket of toys and

---

Signs with store hours

Numeral stamps and ink pads to label food prices

Play money and cash register

Grocery store ads

## Restaurant play

Cookbooks for the chefs

Menus

Magnetic letters and board to post specials

Place mats (cover construction paper with the name of the restaurant written on it; then cover in clear plastic adhesive)

Notepads and pencils for taking orders and writing checks

Play money and cash register

Open and Closed signs

Business Hours sign

## Transportation play

Books for reading in the airport or train station or while riding on the plane or train

Books (Fodor style) about traveling to various destinations

Paper tickets

Maps or an atlas

Suitcases with luggage tags

Travel brochures

Little notebooks for record keeping

## Post office play

Zip code directory

Address book (placed in house play area for use in letter writing during a unit on the post office )

Envelopes of various sizes

Stationery supplies and pencils

Stickers or gummed stamps

Ink pad and stamp to cancel postage stamps

## Office play

Telephone book

Children's picture dictionary

Typewriter or computer terminal and paper

Ledger sheets

Dictation pads and other notepads

Three-ring binders filled with information

Sales brochures

Business cards made from file cards or pieces of tagboard

Filing supplies (folders and a box)

Date stamp and other stamps; an ink pad

books for infants provided in the play doctor's office. Once in a while she puts the book down beside her chair and gets the baby's bottle from the bag that she packed before leaving the house area. She alternates feeding and reading to her baby while she waits for her baby's appointment.

These two children, like most of their preschool peers, have become deeply involved in dramatic play. When books are among the materials one would find in a real-world setting, they should be provided for play in a classroom simulation of the setting. Cookbooks and telephone books can be placed in the house area; little storybooks to read to babies can be placed in a house area or doctor's office; books for adult passengers and their children can be provided for train and plane rides. All of the common dramatic play themes— house, store, doctor's office, business office, airport or train station, fire station, post office—can incorporate books and other print props. Ideas for print props, other than books, that might be included in various dramatic play themes for young children are listed in the box "Literacy Props for Dramatic Play" on pages 92 and 93.

Dramatic play around a certain theme can be prompted by a setting and props: in the house area, dishes, dolls, and dress-up typically engage children in house play. Even within a theme the type of props influence the plots played by the children: dishes, kitchen appliances, and a table and chairs lead to cooking and eating; dolls and doll clothes lead to parenting and dressing; brooms, a dustpan, and empty cleaning containers lead to sweeping and dusting.

The variety of props can influence the complexity of play. For example, a dishcloth, a scouring pad, an empty dish-detergent bottle, a dish rack, and a dish towel are likely to result in a wider range of dishwashing behaviors than would occur if only dishes and a sink were provided. The same is true for print props, and they will be more appreciated and more extensively used if they are added a few at a time.

One way to provide for sustained dramatic play is to start with a skeleton setup and then add props gradually to keep the play area interesting. Noticing that the children in the house area pretended there was a fire and called the fire station, the teacher brings an emergency number decal to attach to the phone on the following day. Or if shopping trips have become popular in house play, the addition of notepads and pencils are likely to maintain and extend the children's interest.

New props can be placed in a play area for children to discover without comment from the teacher. Alternatively, the teacher can explain a prop's use when she gives it to the children: "I thought you might like these notepads to make lists for your shopping trips." Or the teacher might join the play (take on a role) for the purpose of demonstrating a prop's use. Morrow (1990) found that explanations and demonstrations of print props increased

A typewriter is one of many literacy-related props that stimulate children's exploration of print and its functions.

children's use of them in their play. Whatever the method of introduction, children are likely to use a prop in a number of ingenious ways. These innovations can be respected, as long as they make a positive contribution to the play.

Taking children on trips before a particular dramatic play theme is introduced in the classroom shows children how print props are used in a particular setting. While on the trip, the teacher can point out print items as well as other objects so the children can see how people use them. For example, if the receptionist in a doctor's office is writing names in an appointment book, the teacher might ask her to explain what she is doing.

## Summary

In this chapter, various aspects of children's practice at reading have been discussed. Characteristics of the children, characteristics of a range of print materials to be made available to the children, and characteristics of the interactions between adults and children have been considered. Providing children with extensive exposure to books and print props during their preschool years gives them many opportunities to practice reading. Opportunities to practice reading should continue during the kindergarten year.

One of the recommendations for practice made by the Committee on the Prevention of Reading Difficulties in Young Children is that "initial reading instruction" should provide children with "frequent and intensive opportunities to read" (Snow, Burns, & Griffin 1998, 3). If teachers and parents of preschool children provide for such practice, and if they furnish a balanced literacy program in which children come to understand such things as the alphabetic principle, then children are likely to enter first grade with a background that enables them to take advantage of the begining reading instruction offered there.

## References

Clark, M.M. 1976. *Young fluent readers*. Cleveland: Collins.

Durkin, D. 1966. *Children who read early*. New York: Teachers College Press.

Ehri, L.C., & J. Sweet. 1991. Fingerpoint-reading of memorized text: What enables beginners to process the print? *Reading Research Quarterly* 26 (4): 443–62.

Morrow, L.M. 1990. Preparing the classroom environment to promote literacy during play. *Early Childhood Research Quarterly* 5: 537–54.

Morrow, L.M. 1993. *Literacy development in the early years*. Boston: Allyn & Bacon.

Peterson, C.L., & A. McCabe. 1992. Parental styles of narrative elicitation: Effect on children's narrative structure and content. *First Language* 12: 299–321.

Peterson, C.L., & A. McCabe. 1994. A social interactionist account of developing decontextualized narrative skill. *Developmental Psychology* 30 (6): 937–48.

Rawson, R.M., & E.M. Goetz. 1983. Reading-related behavior in preschoolers: Environmental factors and teacher modeling. Unpublished manuscript.

Rossman, F. 1980. Preschoolers' knowledge of the symbolic function of written language in storybooks. Unpublished doctoral dissertation, Boston University.

Snow, C.E., M.S. Burns, & P. Griffin, eds. 1998. *Preventing reading difficulties in young children*. Washington, DC: National Academy Press.

Sulzby, E. 1985. Children's emergent reading of favorite storybooks: A developmental study. *Reading Research Quarterly* 20 (4): 458–81.

Taylor, D. 1983. *Family literacy: Young children learning to read*. Portsmouth, NH: Heinemann.

Learning to write is a very long journey that begins in childhood.

# Young Children and Writing

**5**

A 3-year-old accompanies his mother to the bank. She sits him on the counter while she fills out a savings withdrawal slip. The child watches intently and then asks, "What you doing, Mommy?"

The mother replies, "I'm writing on this form so the cashier will know how much money I want to withdraw from my account."

"I want to write one."

"Okay, here, you can take this one home. We'll write on it there. Other people need to use the counter now, and we are in the way."

The child holds on tightly to the withdrawal slip. At home, his mother gives him a pencil, and he writes on the form. When he shows it to his mother, she says, "Oh, let's see, you need five dollars. OK. 1, 2, 3, 4, 5. Thank you." The mother makes motions as if placing money in the child's hand.

\* \* \*

As this episode suggests, preschoolers are fascinated with writing, with the tools used to do it, with the purposes for which it is used, and with the physical and social results of their own efforts. Many parents know how much young children love to write; they keep writing tools out of the reach of their very young children unless they can supervise their play. Parents know that if they don't watch as children use these fascinating materials, the products of the child's explorations are likely to end up as decorations on walls, magazines, tables, and the floor.

Learning how to write involves much more than learning to form alphabet letters. It involves understanding

1. the level of speech alphabet letters represent;
2. the ways in which print is organized on a page;
3. the purposes for which writing is used;
4. the various conventions associated with various purposes; and
5. that the writer must think about the reader's reaction to the writing.

All of these understandings depend on sophisticated and complex thinking, much of which is beyond a preschooler's abilities. In fact, learning about styles and conventions will occupy children during much of their elementary and secondary school years.

Learning to write is a very long journey. In this chapter, we consider the beginning steps of that journey taken by young children, and how teachers and parents can help them as they make their way.

## Getting writing to look like writing

Children first learn of writing when they see it displayed in their environment and when they see people use writing in a variety of contexts. By the age of 3, children often try to create and organize marks to look like writing. It takes several years for children to learn how to make their individual marks closely resemble standard alphabet letters. It takes about as long for them to learn specific details about how writing is organized on a page. Long before their writing takes on these conventional characteristics, children write in their own unique way.

### *Making marks: From scribble to alphabet letters*

If children are provided with marking tools, a suitable surface on which to apply them, and a safe place to play, they begin to make marks at quite an early age. Case studies have found that children begin to explore with a pencil or crayon sometime between 18 and 24 months of age ( Gardner 1980; Baghban 1984; Schickedanz 1990). Their early markings are experiments: "If I move the crayon this way, what will be the result?" "If I go around this way, what will happen?" They sometimes make patches of marks of one kind and then a new patch of a different kind. A child named Adam experimented in this way between the ages of 18 and 24 months (Figure 5-1).

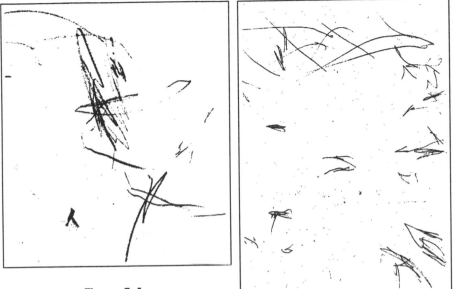

**Figure 5-1.**

Howard Gardner observed that, at 23 months of age, his son Jeremy "possessed a series of schemes or 'moves' in the graphic sphere: he could run through circular motions, dotted patterns, twisted writing like lines." Gardner also observed that none of these remained "at a point of equilibrium or stasis." Instead, Jeremy's "activity progressed every day" (1980, 25–26).

The progress made by very young children indicates that they watch closely the lines resulting from a movement, that they study carefully the relationship between movement and lines, and that they deliberately vary their actions. Eleanor Gibson commented quite a number of years ago that although "scribbling seems to be its own reward . . . it furnishes an unparalleled opportunity for learning the relations between the finger movements that guide the tool and the resulting visual feedback" (1975, 293). Lines are lines, no matter the purpose for which they are created. Thus, this early scribbling tutors children and aids their writing.

**Early scribble writing.** Children's first marks are scribbles. They create many different kinds. Some scribbles are organized so as to resemble pictures; others look more like writing. Writing-like scribbles may be linear rather than circular, and they may be arranged horizontally more than vertically. They also may contain repetitions of a particular kind of line segment. Children use these organizational characteristics to create their first writing, and they use the same characteristics to judge whether visual displays they are shown are writing as opposed to pictures (Lavine 1977).

Although children's scribble writing lacks many of the characteristics we find in conventional writing, there is something very print-like, rather than picture-like, about it.

We can see quite clearly that children distinguish between pictures and print, and therefore between drawing and writing, when we look at a sample of each produced by the same child on the same piece of paper. Nora's pictures of a butterfly and her story about it appear in Figure 5-2. The part Nora said was her story certainly looks like writing, instead of like pictures, even though the writing contains no recognizable letters.

Harste, Burke, and Woodward (1981) obtained many examples of such differentiation in a study in which they asked children first to draw a picture of themselves and then to sign it with their name (Figure 5-3).

Another example of a child's ability to create contrast between picture and scribble writing, created by my son Adam, is shown in Figure 5-4. The picture fills most of the page. When asked to tell about "the small, wavy lines, over here" (lower right side), Adam said, "Those are words. Just words."

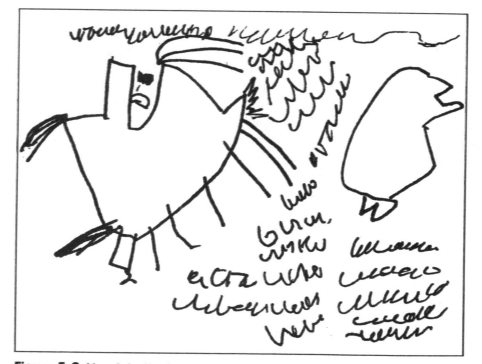

**Figure 5-2.** Nora's butterfly and her story (Schickedanz & Hultz 1979).

**Figure 5-3.** A picture (top) and the artist's signature (bottom), produced by a 3-year-old (Harste, Burke, & Woodward 1981, 421).

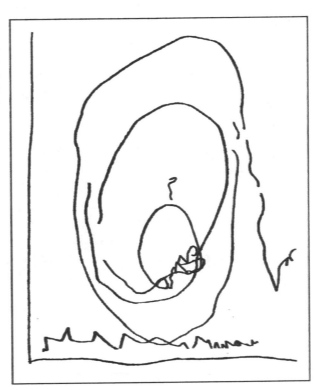

**Figure 5-4.** Adam's scribble writing is tucked under the lower right portion of his scribble drawing (Schickedanz, personal collection).

> The initial letter of the child's name is often the first letter she is able to make.

**A few letters appear.** As children gain experience with writing, they usually begin to write actual alphabet letters, or close approximations of them, even though they still tend to use scribble much of the time. Often the two kinds of marks are combined in one writing composition, as in the case of Emma's writing, which appears in Figure 5-5. A perfectly formed uppercase *E* appears in Emma's writing sample, as does another form that appears *E*-like. Perhaps with this latter form, Emma was conducting an experiment with the lines used to make uppercase *E*s.

The writing sample created by Tawanna is similar in that it too contains a few well formed letters plus scribble (Figure 5-6). In Tawanna's sample, the letter is *T.* In both samples, the letter the child included was the first letter of her name. It is quite common to find a letter from the child's name mixed in with the child's scribble writing (Clay 1975).

**Figure 5-5.** Emma, age 4 years (Schickedanz & Molina 1979).

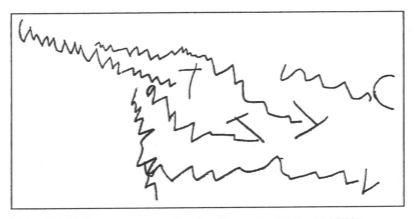

**Figure 5-6.** Tawanna, age 3 years, 2 months (Holland 1982).

**Mock letters.** As children gain more knowledge about how lines can be combined to form letters, their writing contains fewer scribble marks and more marks that are *mock letters* (letter-like forms) (Clay 1975). Mock letters are not actual letters, but they look a lot like them because they are made from the same set of line segments. Writing samples made primarily of mock letters often contain a few actual letters as well. Samples of mock writing are shown in Figures 5-7 and 5-8. Figure 5-7 is a shopping list. Figure 5-8 is the story *The Three Bears*, which this child wrote for her mother. Actual letters can be found in both writing samples, although mock letters are more numerous.

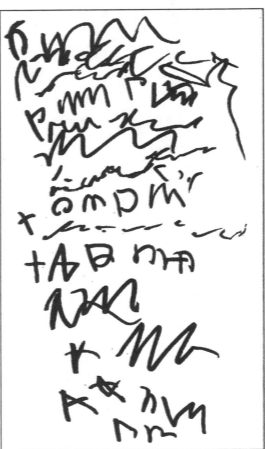

**Figure 5-7.** Andy, age 4. A shopping list. This writing contains mock cursive and mock manuscript letters (Schickedanz, personal collection).

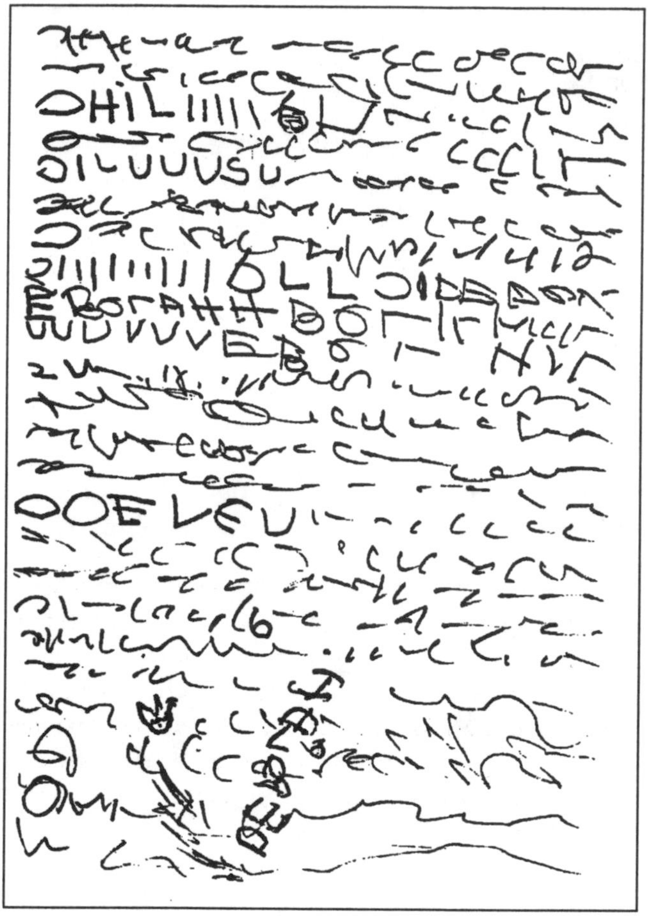

**Figure 5-8.** The story of *The Three Bears*, written by a 4 ½-year-old (Schickedanz & Sullivan 1984).

**Writing with and practicing letters.** The writing in Figures 5-9 and 5-10 shows some progress beyond the mock writing in Figures 5-7 and 5-8. Only actual letters appear in these samples, although the letters contain characteristic errors. The orientation of some letters, the number of lines found in certain letters, and the child's accuracy in making lines touch one another

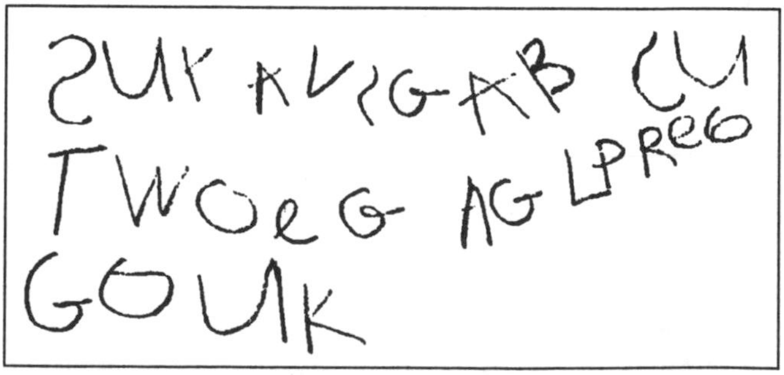

**Figure 5-9.** Writing produced by a 5-year-old (Schickedanz & Waldorf 1980).

**Figure 5-10.** Writing produced by a 5-year-old (Schickedanz & Sullivan 1984).

are not yet under complete control. Control over these features will emerge as the child continues to write and as the child makes use of demonstrations and suggestions provided by adults at home and at child care.

Some children seem to work actively to perfect various letters. They conduct experiments on one letter only or on a few. Sometimes a child seems to take a letter to the extreme, perhaps by crossing one line with another or by shortening and then lengthening a line. Paulette (Figure 5-11) seems to have done this sort of experimenting with lowercase *t*. We can see that she varied her *t*s in various ways: the position at which the top horizontal line intersects the vertical line, the lengths of both the horizontal and vertical lines, and the orientation of the entire unit.

**Figure 5-11.** Paulette's display of her *t*s (Schickedanz & Molina 1979).

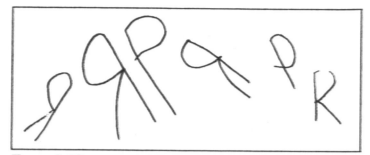

**Figure 5-12.** An experiment with the letter *R*. Richard, age 3 years, 8 months (Holland 1982).

Richard (Figure 5-12) seems to have conducted a similar experiment. The letter *R* was on his mind. Richard may have forgotten to add a line to an *R* in two instances, or he might have been trying to see in what ways a capital *R* and a capital *P* are the same and different.

Sometimes, instead of taking one letter to its limits in various ways, children compare similar letters. An experiment of this kind can be seen in Figure 5-13. A child wrote several letters containing only straight vertical and horizontal lines.

**Figure 5-13.** (Clay 1975, 42)

### Choosing from a writing repertoire

Even after children are able to produce writing that resembles standard writing very closely, they often use scribble or mock writing. Figure 5-14 shows the scribble writing of a 4½-year-old. The child who produced it had been given a small notebook and a clipboard to take along to meetings she attended quite often with her mother. Her mother usually did a lot of writing at these meetings. The child became interested in writing too and always took her supplies along. When she produced this sample, the child could

**Figure 5-14.** Scribble writing created by a 4½-year-old imitating her mother's note taking at a meeting (Schickedanz & Sullivan, unpublished data).

write her name in standard form and could write MOM and DAD. But when she wanted to produce a lot of writing—imitate an adult while writing or produce cursive writing—she often created scribble writing rather than standard writing.

A 4½-year-old might write his name very carefully using quite well formed alphabet letters when signing a painting or a drawing. But the next minute, when playing in the classroom house area, the same child might scribble write a shopping list. Different times, different places, different purposes, with writing to match each one.

This behavior is quite typical. Young children do not discard earlier forms of writing altogether when they become capable of creating more mature forms. For a while they produce them all, selecting from among their expanding repertoire the kind of writing that serves them best in each situation.

## Learning to write alphabet letters

When children produce scribble pictures in which they repeat the same kind of line a number of times, we see evidence of children trying to understand "the relations between the finger movements that guide the tool and the resulting visual feedback" (Gibson 1975, 293). In Figure 5-15, for example, we can see several zigzag lines and a patch of dots. There are two patches of

Exploration with a writing tool enables children to learn about the relation between hand movement and various kinds of marks.

**Figure 5-15.** A drawing by a 23-month-old (Schickedanz, personal collection).

lines created by moving the marker back and forth. There are also three enclosed figures, at the upper right, and four diagonal lines intersecting a horizontal line. Exploration with a writing tool enables children to learn about the relation between hand movements and various kinds of marks.

Writing alphabet letters requires several kinds of knowledge: (1) a good visual image of each letter (that is, knowing how each letter looks), (2) knowledge of the line segments used to form each letter, (3) knowledge about the sequence in which the lines are put together to compose the letter, and (4) knowledge about the direction in which to draw each of the lines. What is the source of each kind of knowledge? What can teachers and parents do to help children acquire it? See the box titled "Helping Young Children Learn to Form Letters" (pp. 110–111) for a discussion of ways in which teachers can help young children learn to write alphabet letters.

*A brief caveat:* The wise teacher is reluctant to provide formal instruction in handwriting to groups of preschool and kindergarten children. Instead, she provides paper and marking tools for children to explore writing. Teachers are concerned—and with good reason—that if they regularly provide formal and direct instruction to preschool and kindergarten classes, children's interest in writing may be undermined. Nevertheless, the thoughtful teacher takes advantage of opportunities to demonstrate writing and help individual children as the need arises.

# *H*elping Young Children Learn to Form Letters

## A good visual image of each letter

Looking at letters enables children to distinguish between them and learn their features. Because some letters differ only slightly, children need experiences in which they can compare letters directly to each other. The teacher can provide alphabet matching games and puzzles to help children acquire this knowledge. Seeing alphabet letters in familiar words, such as their name, also helps children learn to identify letters. Exposure to alphabet books can help as well.

## Line segments

Looking at a letter gives the child some information about the line segments used in forming that letter. Children are more apt to notice specific lines when teachers write each line segment of a letter in a different color when making alphabet-letter matching materials. Children can then see that there is one horizontal line rather than two across the top of uppercase *T*, for example, and that uppercase *E* is not composed of one continuous line to form the upper, left side, and lower portions but one long vertical line with three short horizontal lines attached to it. However, simply looking at already formed letters is not sufficient.

When children can watch as a letter is written, they gain much more information about the lines used to form that letter. The teacher can provide demonstrations by playing an alphabet clue game with a small group of children: the teacher writes an alphabet letter, one line at a time, on a large piece of chart paper and asks children which letter they think she has mind. If she draws a long vertical line, children might guess *T* or perhaps *H, E, or F*–all are plausible guesses. The teacher continues by adding another line. If she's making an uppercase *T*, the second line will be the last clue. However, if she has in mind *E*, the children might guess *F*. A child might guess *T* if he is confused about how many lines form the horizontal bar of an uppercase *T*. If a child says *T*, the teacher might take a moment to demonstrate on another piece of paper how to form an uppercase *T*. Some children might guess *L* because an uppercase $L$ is made of a vertical and a horizontal line segment. In this case, the teacher might say, "Well, that's a good guess, but I would have put the short line down here if I'd had an $L$ in mind. The teacher adds lines until the chosen letter is formed and the children have identified it.

Wise teachers don't overdo the use of such games; playing them only once in a while keeps children's interest high. Teachers may find that children initiate the games with each other when they are gathered at the writing area.

## The sequence and direction of the lines that form letters

The sequence and direction of drawing the lines to form a letter cannot be discerned from looking at already formed letters nor easily grasped from worksheets with arrows and numbers marking lines in a model letter; they are best learned by watching demonstrations. The alphabet clue game already discussed informs children about the sequence in which lines are drawn and about the direction. Children can also be shown individually how to follow letter guides as the teacher uses them to provide demonstrations in response to queries about letter formation.

When letter guides on strips (designed for attaching to classroom tabletops) are mounted on a tagboard square and laminated, several individual letter-writing reference guides can be made available and placed on a shelf in the classroom writing center. A teacher can use one of these guides as she responds to questions, pointing out how the guide helps her remember which line to draw first, second, and so on, and in which direction to draw each one. Children will soon begin to go to the guides themselves rather than request help from the teacher.

The large, wall alphabet charts have the disadvantage of being far removed from the child and the teacher. It is difficult for a young child to look at a chart in the distance, look down at his own writing, glance back to the chart for the next bit of information, then again to his own writing. Nor can the wall chart be moved to the writing table where a child can inspect a letter closely and follow the numbers and arrows more easily. Preschool and kindergarten teachers might want to dispense with the large, wall alphabet charts altogether and provide instead a number of smaller ones that can literally get into a child's hands.

Teachers also have a chance to provide demonstrations of letter formation in authentic tasks–when the class writes a thank-you letter, for example, or creates an experience chart following a class field trip. Children dictate the message, and the teacher writes it down while they watch. The teacher can sometimes describe her actions as she draws the lines to form various letters. This description draws children's attention to the letter-forming actions and helps them remember the actions to perform when writing that letter themselves.

## *Fine-motor development and handwriting*

Fine-motor development involves the skillful use of the fingers in manipulating different objects. The various immature grasps familiar to preschool and kindergarten teachers have been studied and described by a number of researchers (for example, Carlson & Cunningham 1990). At first young children usually use a fist grasp. The hand grips the crayon stiffly, and the whole arm is held above the tabletop. The movement guiding the hand across the paper comes from the muscle in the upper arm. Various overhand and stiff finger grips usually follow the fist grip before children adopt a more mature grip, using the index and middle fingers plus the thumb. In a mature grip, the side of the hand rests on the tabletop. This takes the weight off the point of the writing tool and allows for flexible movement of the tool as it is held by fingers and thumb.

As long as the movement of the writing or drawing tool comes from movement of the muscle in the upper arm, the marks the child makes will be relatively large and crude due to the great distance between the pivot and the point of the writing tool—the child is unable to control the movements very well. When the child holds the writing tool in her fingers, the point of control is much closer to the end of the writing tool, and the child is able to make smaller marks.

Making controlled movements and precise lines is usually difficult for many young children, given their fine-motor limitations. Even children with considerable knowledge about how specific alphabet letters look and how to put lines together to make them can lack the fine-motor skills necessary to form letters that look like the images in their mind. Children themselves sometimes notice that their creations do not match their intentions. Their frustration is heightened when specific expectations are held for preschool and kindergarten children; therefore, it is probably best for teachers to provide opportunities for children to learn how to form letters without requiring them to participate in formal handwriting instruction.

Handwriting instruction is at first aimed at helping children print. Instruction in cursive writing is typically not begun until second or even third grade, in part because the circular movements required are difficult for a child to make until the cartilage in the wrist has turned to bone (Berk 1996). This process, known as *ossification*, is under the control of maturation. In most children, ossification in the wrist is not complete until around the age of 6 (Berk 1996).

## Organizing writing on a page

Another aspect of learning to write is learning how to organize writing on the paper. This task is not as easy as it may seem because it entails an understanding of spatial concepts.

In much of children's early writing, vertical and horizontal placement are mixed. For example, while both Emma and Tawanna (Figures 5-5 and 5-6) mainly used horizontally arranged scribble segments, they created vertically placed segments as well. Moreover, in many of the writing examples we have already considered, orientation of the letters themselves is not consistent. Sometimes letters are reversed; sometimes, as in Tawanna's sample, they are placed upside down. These characteristics, plus a tendency to write in any direction—left to right, right to left, top to bottom, bottom to top— are all related.

Until children understand that space can be organized in terms of coordinates, they do not select any consistent direction in which to place their writing, nor do they orient letters consistently. Mixed orientations are often found within the same writing sample. For example, when Sharon (Figure 5-16) ran out of room on her small piece of paper after she wrote "I love you," she simply rotated the paper 180° and wrote "Sharon," left to right, under her message. She did not seem to notice that her completed sample contained two rows of writing whose orientations were inconsistent.

**Figure 5-16.** (Schickedanz & Molina 1979).

**Figure 5-17.**
Terrence, age 6
years (Holland
1982).

Terrence (Figure 5-17), on the other hand, knew how to solve the problem of running out of space on a line: go to the left and begin another.

Sometimes when children write from right to left, they reverse each letter perfectly, as well, so that the writing produced is a mirror image of the standard left-to-right form (Figure 5-18). This kind of error shows a violation of accepted writing conventions (social agreements about the direction of writing) but a good understanding of spatial relations. It takes considerable skill to keep directions and orientations consistent within a sample of writing the way this child did. A child once said to me, "Okay, I'm going to write my name forwards, and then I'm going to write it backwards." He proceeded to do just that.

**Figure 5-18.** Mirror-image writing produced by Claire, age 5 years, 6 months (Holland 1982).

Children who are as skilled as these two children clearly know that there are two distinct directions in which to write. They have good control over both of them. They are probably ready to be reminded that "we write from left to right" in situations where such a reminder is appropriate. Of course, it is not appropriate when a child is playing with the direction of writing, as was the case with the second child discussed above.

Another aspect of learning to organize writing on a page involves leaving a space between words. Young children tend to run words together when they write. They probably lack knowledge about what, in some cases, constitutes a word in speech. Compare the words *today* and *to go*. It would not be clear to a child that one word is involved in the first instance while two

> Children's errors often show us what they know about the conventions of writing, as well as what they have not yet learned.

words are involved in the second. Second, young children lack appreciation for the difficulty readers will have deciphering what is written, having no prior knowledge of the message. It's easier to read *I want a cat for my birthday* when it is written in standard form than when it is written like this: IWATACT4MYBRTHDA. Finally, young children no doubt simply lack knowledge about this writing convention. No one has specifically told them that space should be left between words.

A child who understands the first two conditions but not the last one often creates some way to separate words. For example, Paul, whose writing appears in Figure 5-19, used a dot to separate each word. Other children use dashes or slashes. If children create such devices, we can be quite sure they will understand what we are talking about when we tell them space is used to separate one word from another.

Again, it is not necessary to fuss at young children when they want to experiment with word dividers of their own making. Slashes, dashes, and dots work just fine for a while. After children have played around with these devices, they usually adopt the convention of leaving spaces.

**Figure 5-19.** Paul, age 5 years, 8 months. (Reprinted by permission of the publisher from GYNS AT WRK by Glenda L. Bissex, Cambridge, Mass.: Harvard University Press, Copyright © 1980 by the President and Fellows of Harvard College.)

# Learning that alphabet letters represent speech at the phoneme level

Suppose we found ourselves in the midst of a society without a written language and someone asked us to create one. First, we would need to decide at what level our orthography (writing system) would represent the oral language. Would we create a *logography*–an orthography that represents speech at the word level? Would we create a *syllabary*–an orthography that represents speech at the syllable level? Or would we create an *alphabetic orthography*–a writing system that represents individual sounds or phonemes?

Languages using all of these systems exist in the world. The writing system used to represent Chinese is a logography. Each character stands for one object, action, or idea. Learning the symbols in this kind of writing system is a matter of associating a particular design (character) with the object, action, or idea it represents. Each character is unique: it is used to represent just one object, action, or idea.

The orthography used to represent Japanese is a syllabary. Syllables are combined in various ways to create all of the words in the language. This is a sound-based system, not a visual system like a logography. English, French, Russian, and Spanish orthographies are alphabetic. Alphabet letters are used to represent *individual* sounds in words.

Each type of writing system has advantages and disadvantages. For example, the units of speech represented by logographies and syllabaries are easier to hear. When the units are easier to hear, it is easier for children to understand the basic way in which these writing systems work. However, when unique characters are used to write each word, a person must learn a large number of symbols. For example, there are about 70,000 characters used to write in Chinese (Taylor 1981).

A syllabary needs far fewer symbols than a logography, but the number is still large compared with the number of alphabet letters used in an alphabetic orthography. In English, learning just 26 unique letters allows one to write any English word.

The disadvantage of an alphabetic orthography is that the unit of speech represented by alphabet letters is not easy to find and isolate (Liberman et al. 1974). As we discussed in Chapter 3, the individual-sound level of language–the phoneme–is not what we ordinarily think about when conversing. As Menyuk (1976) explained, in "real speech processing" the focus is on words and on relations between words because this is where meaning is to be found. Because *conscious* phonemic analysis is not required to any great extent in oral language processing, children are not accustomed to thinking about speech at this level. Moreover, many phonemic elements, as we come to think of them for the purpose of representing each with an alphabet let-

When the child holds the writing tool in her fingers, the point of control is much closer to the end of the writing tool, and the child can make smaller marks.

ter, do not exist in pure form in the stream of real speech. We learn to *think about* words in terms of individual sounds, but demarcations between these individual sounds are blurred in actual speech. Even when we try to sound out words, it is difficult to emit one sound in isolation.

When children learn to write, they must come to understand how their writing system works at this very basic level. This is not an easy task. As we discussed in Chapter 3, oral language experiences with rhyme and alliteration probably set the stage for the development of the heightened sensitivity to language at the phonemic level that is required for children to be able to spell words or know what to do with the series of sounds they end up with after sounding out letters in a printed word. Specific experiences with segmentation of speech are also necessary for the development of phonemic segmentation ability (that is, the ability to work one's way through a word, from start to finish, isolating each phoneme in turn).

# Children's early hypotheses about how words are created

Long before children have even an inkling about how the writing system actually works, they write using first one hypothesis and then another. Gradually, through their own observations and tutoring from adults, their understanding increases.

## *Visual hypotheses*

The first information children have about words is how they look. At first, children have no idea that the way a written word looks depends on the sequence of sounds we hear when we say the words. Because children do not know that the writing system is sound based, their first hypotheses about words are completely visually based.

Children's very first visual hypothesis is also influenced by their knowledge of symbolization. In the case of pictures and of objects used in pretend play, the representation resembles in some physical way the object or person represented. Children do not know that writing does not work in this way—that writing is an arbitrary symbol system (that is, the symbols bear no physical relationship to the things they represent).

**Hypothesis: Words are related physically to what they represent.** Children's very first idea about how to write the name of an object or person is that it works something like making a picture of the thing. Children know from their observations of writing that features of a person or object are not included in the way they are when we draw a picture of them. However, young children think that *something* about the physical characteristics of people or objects must be captured when their names are written. Children capture this physical aspect of a person or an object in its name by using more characters for a larger object or person and fewer characters for a smaller one (Papandropoulou & Sinclair 1974; Ferreiro & Teberosky 1982; Schickedanz 1990).

To give up this hypothesis, children would need to be informed about specific printed words and the objects or persons these words represent. For example, if a child's mother's name is Ana and the child's name is Christopher, and the child saw both names in print and knew to which person each belonged, he would receive information about writing that contradicts this hypothesis. Similarly, if the child saw labels under pictures in books and someone read them to him, the child would see that the grasshopper has a fairly long name while the lion has a short one. It would take several in-

> At first, children have no idea that the way a written word looks depends on the sequence of sounds we hear when we say the word.

stances such as this, over a period of time, for the child to realize that writing must work differently than he first supposed.

Groups of children who have been observed using this hypothesis about writing ranged in age from 3 to 5 or 6 years. This wide range in ages can perhaps be best explained by taking into account variations in children's experiences. It is very doubtful that characteristics of the group of children themselves account for this wide variation. It is more likely that some groups of children have many socially mediated experiences with print at a fairly young age, while others do not. Unless someone reads words to a child and helps the child link them to objects and people, that child is not likely to give up this hypothesis very quickly. We can see here an example of how children's literacy learning depends on social interaction with adults.

**Hypothesis: Writing consists of arbitrary visual designs.** When children realize that the selection of characters for writing a word does not depend on establishing a physical relationship between the object and the word, they understand that writing is arbitrary. However, they still have no idea *why* specific letters are selected. In fact, they think that each word's *design* (sequence of letters) is unique and must be learned.

Children have no idea, at this early phase in their understanding of writing, that a small set of 26 alphabet letters is used to write all words. This is why we hear 3-year-olds, and sometimes 4-year-olds as well, say, "Hey, that's my name!" when they see *any* word beginning with the first letter of their name. If two or three children in a preschool class have names starting with the same letter, they might mistake each others' names for their own. Teachers find themselves saying, "Yes, Juanita, your name starts with *J* just like Jose's, but your name doesn't have an *s* in the middle. It has an *n* and a *t*. Your name is just like Jose's at the beginning, but your names have different letters after that."

Experiences such as this one are required for children to learn that the same letters appear in many different words, that both the arrangement of letters and the particular collection of letters used make words different, even though many of the same characters also appear in different words. It is extremely helpful if adults comment about this feature of words. For example, in one preschool class there was a child named Tyler and another named Taylor. When a child in the class was confused about which name was which, a teacher helped the child compare them, directing the child's attention to the *a* in the second position in Taylor's name and the *y* in the second position in Tyler's.

Another situation that rather naturally brings this basic fact about an alphabetic writing system to children's attention is one in which magnetic alphabet letters are provided on a large magnetic board. Even when several sets are provided, some children inevitably can't find a specific letter they need to write their own names because other children who are playing with the magnetic letters have already used it. Inevitably a child in need of a specific letter says, "But that's mine!" A child who has already used the letter says, "No, it's mine!" A teacher can come to the rescue and explain, "Actually, both of your names have the letter *t,* and so does Anthony's. Here, I'll make another *t* on a piece of paper, and we can stick a little magnetic tape on the back. Then there will be enough *t*s for everyone to use."

**Hypothesis: Letter strings are based on visual rules.** Children move to a higher level of understanding about writing once they have the idea that alphabet letters are used over and over to create many different words. When this idea dawns, children begin to create mock words. *Mock words* look like actual words because children capture some basic characteristics of how words look (Figure 5-20). Words cannot be too long or too short (3 to 6 or 7 characters), not because words are never that long or short but because most words children see do not fall outside that range. Children also know that the number of successive repetitions of the same letter within

**Figure 5-20.** The 4-year-old creator of these mock words followed several rules: (1) use multiple letters but not too many; (2) reorder the same letters to create different words; and (3) repeat the same letter only twice in succession.

a word cannot exceed two. Children know as well that the very same letters can be rearranged to make different words.

Of course, what children do not know is that arrangements of letters meeting these visual criteria do not always turn out to be actual words. A sequence of letters can look like words are supposed to look but still not be an actual word. Only when the letters are selected so as to correspond to the sounds we hear in a word as we say it will the sequence of letters turn out to be an actual word.

When children create a mock word, they typically take it to an adult and ask, "What word is this?" Adults often sound out the letter sequence the child has written. When the result does not resemble an actual word, children usually laugh as they realize that a real word has not been spoken. Many children engage in this kind of word-writing play for several months. At some point they seem to realize that this way of going about trying to write words simply does not work. They stop creating mock words and begin to ask adults for spellings. Or they copy known words from print they see in the classroom.

### *The transition from visual hypotheses to sound-based hypotheses*

Children may already have attempted to code the sound of words before or while creating mock words. If children make a sound-based attempt at writing this early, they typically code with one mark each "beat" (syllable) heard in a word. Perhaps they have gotten the basic idea that the sound structure of a word must be captured in some way when we write it, if someone has written words for them while stressing the syllables. For example, if writing *Adam,* the child's name, the adult might say, "Aaaaa [while writing A]–dam[while writing d-a-m]." If provided demonstrations of this kind, a child would surely notice that writing captures the sound of words in some way. But sound at the *phoneme* level eludes the child until demonstrations provided by adults segment words at this level of speech.

A child often catches on to this level of sound coding when she asks an adult to spell a word and the adult, as she writes, talks out loud in a way that allows the child to see and hear the adult's thinking. Instead of simply dictating letters needed to spell the word or writing the word for the child to copy, the adult sounds out the word, phoneme by phoneme, while dictating the letter used to code it. The child might do the writing to the best of her ability, but the adult is generating the word's spelling. When words do not contain a one-to-one match of phonemes to graphemes, which is the case very often in English, the adult can say, "There's an *e* on the end, but we don't hear it" when providing the spelling for *kite,* for example.

If children know letter names, they soon begin to join in to dictate the letters needed to spell a phoneme after the adult isolates it. (See "Teaching the Alphabet in Authentic Contexts," pp. 146–147, in Chapter 6.) Children need a lot of experience with phonemic segmentation demonstrations before they are able to pick up this part of the spelling process. They notice and can isolate easier-to-hear phonemes first—often at the beginning of words or at the end. Gradually they develop skill in working their way through entire words. This level of phonemic segmentation skill is rarely seen in preschoolers, although it has been observed by various researchers (for example, Read 1975). Typically children reach this level during the kindergarten or first-grade year.

The particular age at which a child achieves this level of skill depends greatly on the child's experiences. Early experience with rhyme and alliteration seem to help. Later, hearing adults demonstrate segmentation is also vital. Ideally these experiences occur when the child asks for a spelling. Once the child has some budding skill in segmentation, we see independent attempts to spell words.

**Phoneme-level invented spellings.** Children who invent spellings segment words into their constituent phonemes and code each one with an alphabet letter. Because children are not able to hear all of the phonemes in some words, and are not able to represent some they hear in the standard way specified by English orthography, their spellings look odd.

Letter-name knowledge provides children with enough information to begin coding phonemes they isolate. When a letter's name is said, the phoneme it represents is heard. However, in English, there is not a letter-name match for some phonemes. For example, soft or lax vowel phonemes (*A*dam, *a*nother) are not contained in the name of the letter used to represent them, nor is there a letter-name match for phonemes represented by the letter combinations *th, wh,* and *sh.* (A fourth combination, *ch,* actually is heard when the letter *h* is named, but *h* is not used in English orthography to spell this phoneme. Because children use letter names to find letter-phoneme matches, they sometimes spell *chicken* as HKN and *cherry* as HRE.)

Tense-vowel phonemes—or what are commonly known as long vowels—present little problem to children because vowel letter names contain this phoneme. Children use this letter-name-to-phoneme information in spelling words such as *face* (FAS), *came* (KAM), and *Coke* (KOK) (Read 1975).

The lax, or short, vowels, however, are more difficult. Because there is no letter-name match, children represent each lax vowel with the letter used to represent the tense-vowel phoneme that is most similar to it in terms of place of articulation. To solve lax-vowel phoneme representations, children substitute one vowel grapheme (letter) for another.

# *A*rticulation of /č/, /t(r)/, and /t/ in English.

| Feature | /č/ | /t(r)/ | /t/ | Intrepretation |
|---|---|---|---|---|
| Delayed release | yes | yes | no | (affrication) |
| Anterior | no | no | yes | (place of articulation) |
| Distributed | yes | no | no | (type of contact) |
| Restroflex | no | yes | no | (tongue shape) |

*Adapted from Read, 1975, p. 53. Copyright 1975 by the National Council of Teachers of English. Reprinted with permission.*

For example, children often represent the lax vowel found in words such as *fish, igloo, sink,* and *will* with the letter *e* rather than the letter *i*. When you pronounce the sound represented by the letter *e* in *Eva* and compare it to how your mouth feels when you pronounce the second phoneme in *dike,* you can see why children choose *e* instead of *i* for words like *fish* and *sink.* For the same reason children often represent the middle-vowel phoneme (/ɛ/) in *pen, mess,* or *teddy bear* with the letter *a* (PAN, MAS, TADEBR), and the middle-vowel phoneme (/a/) in *got, box,* and *upon* with the letter *i* (GIT, BIGS, UPIN) (Read 1975).

Additional errors in children's first spellings are due to lack of knowledge about which phonetic features should be given the most weight when deciding how to code a phoneme. The table above compares the features of three sounds, /č/ as in *church,* /t(r)/ as in *trunk,* and /t/ as in *toy.* As the table shows, when the phoneme is followed by an *r,* as in the word *trunk,* it shares the delay release and place of articulation features with the /č/ sound found in *church,* and it shares the distributed feature with the /t/ sound found in *toy.* When forced to choose between the letters *ch* and *t* to represent this phoneme when it appears before an *r,* children often choose *ch.* Thus, they spell words such as *troubles* and *try* like this: CHRIBLES and CHRIE (Read 1975). Such spellings may look funny to us, but they certainly are understandable from a phonetic standpoint!

These various examples illustrate that young children's spelling is not the result of poor listening. In fact, adults need to struggle to think about the sounds and sound relationships children detect. Adults have used standard spelling for so long that the *t* in *truck* and the *t* in *toy* sound very much alike to us, whereas the *ch* in church and the *t* in *truck* sound completely different. This mind-set also makes us think they sound a certain way. But the young child hears them differently because he has not yet learned to filter what is heard through the mind-set of standard spelling.

Clearly, admonishing children to listen carefully as we pronounce words does not really help them solve these problems. Exposing children to standard spellings found in storybooks and on classroom signs, labels, and charts is one way to help young children move in the direction of standard spellings. Helping them with spellings when they request them is another. Short explanations of *why* we chose one alphabet letter rather than another to code a phoneme also provide useful instruction.

Children's own efforts to write the sounds in words as they hear them—their "invented spellings"—help them segment words into phonemes in reading.

For example, if we are using the letter *a* to write the first phoneme in the word again, we can say, after we have isolated this first phoneme, "We use the letter *a* to write that sound. We also use the letter *a* to write the first sound in *acorn*. We can use the letter *a* to write *two* different sounds, just as we use an *i* to write both *Isabel* and *ice cream*. That's how writing works." (All of this might be done in the context of writing down a child's dictation.)

**Does inventing spellings harm children?** Some people feel that permitting children to work out their own spellings is a mistake. They worry that children will get in the habit of spelling words incorrectly and that this might hinder their success in learning to read. There is some reason for concern when children are permitted to invent spellings for several years—perhaps long after they have started elementary school (Stahl, Duffy-Hester, & Stahl 1998). Viewing their own misspellings year after year could interfere with children's acquisition of the visual knowledge about the sequences found in standard English syllables.

On the other hand, children learning to read need to grasp the concept that words are composed of a series of sounds, and they benefit from many opportunities to practice detecting these sounds in the order in which they occur. Trying to spell words presents children with one of the best opportunities to learn to segment words into their constituent phonemes (Adams 1990). Of course, the practice must not be taken to extremes.

An example of taking the invented spelling idea to an extreme is seen when teachers respond to a child's query, "Is this right?" by saying, "Oh, any way you want to write the word will be okay. It doesn't matter." A child who asks such a question probably knows something about how specific words are *supposed* to look and thinks the spelling he has written does not look correct. Dismissing such a question does not show appropriate respect for a child's desire to learn about spelling, nor does it help the child move forward in acquiring this knowledge.

**Phoneme-based spelling combined with orthographic information.** As children see more and more words in various contexts, such as in familiar books and on classroom signs, street signs, food cartons, and classroom materials, they begin to build visual knowledge about how words should look. Often children have learned how to spell a few words correctly by the time they are 4 or 5 years old. In addition to their own name, and perhaps the names of family members or friends, these words might include *yes, no, cat, love, dear,* and other words of special interest to a particular child.

Sometimes, even though children can spell some words, they try instead to sound out these words rather than first think about how they know these words are spelled. When they do this, the sequence of letters they create often does not match the standard spelling they have seen on many different occasions. At this point children often do not know that sounding out to spell is not quite all there is to spelling in English. Viewing the result of their attempt to spell a word they have seen, children wonder just how the word is supposed to be spelled.

Children who find themselves in this situation will often ask adults, "Is this right?" or "Is this how you spell *love?*" If adults wish to be truly helpful to children, they will take such questions seriously. In the event that *love* has been spelled LUV or LV, the teacher can say, "Actually, most people spell *love* l-o-v-e. We don't even hear a sound on the end for the letter *e,* but that's how *love* is spelled. Sometimes it's hard to know how to spell a word. We just need to learn and remember the spelling of some words, or we can ask for help or look at a list."

These conversations occur mostly during a child's kindergarten year or when a child is in first grade. However, sometimes these conversations do occur with preschoolers, especially those who are early readers. Because children who read early have a great deal of visual knowledge about words, they often do not want to generate their own spellings by sounding out unfamiliar words. Adults can help them by sounding out these words and also commenting about and explaining the situation when there is not a one-to-one match between sounds heard in the word and the word's spelling. For example, when spelling *cake,* the adult can explain that the *e* is written at the end not because it represents a sound we hear at the end of the word when we pronounce it; rather, the *e* tells us how to say the *a* used for the middle sound in *cake.* The letter *a* is used to represent more than one sound. It is used in *cat* and *cake.*

Interactions between teachers and children in a preschool classroom are not likely to be dominated by questions about whether a spelling a child has created is right. The most frequent interactions will occur in response to children's requests for spellings, with a child having made no independent attempt. Most preschoolers need the adult to sound out the word—to isolate its phonemes—before they can do so independently.

Children's first independent attempts to isolate phonemes and code them, no matter how far afield, should be allowed to stand because of the practice children acquire in segmenting words into phonemes and in thinking about letter-sound correspondences. Later, when phonemic segmentation of words is well in hand, adults can begin to help children learn standard spellings. This includes helping children gradually get into the habit of using more of these in their writing—even in a first draft. Helping children make the transition from invented to standard spelling is the task of teachers in the primary grades.

## Learning about the many purposes of writing

Suppose you received this imaginary letter in the mail:

Dear Helen,

Once upon a time there was a frog named Hippity-Hop. He lived in a lake and sat on lily pads. One day he fell off of a lily pad, and that was the last time anyone saw him. Too bad!

The End,

Chris

You would probably find such a letter amusing because the style of the writing is characteristic of stories, not personal letters.

Through their experiences with print in various forms, young children become aware of the difference between the form of a letter and that of a story. What is particularly interesting is that we rarely, if ever, receive such a letter, even from a very young child. Apparently, very young children become aware of the difference between the form of a letter and the form of a story fairly quickly if they have been exposed to each.

In addition to knowing what to say when writing a letter versus a story, young children quickly observe that writing is organized differently for different purposes. Children who write lists, for example, place the writing on the paper in a list-like array. When they write a letter or a story, they include more writing on each line (Figure 5-21).

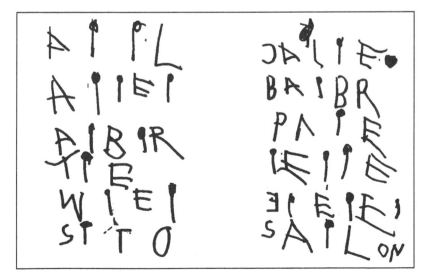

**Figure 5-21.** This grocery list, written by a 4-year-old, is organized as lists are typically organized. Had the child written a letter or story instead, she would have placed writing in longer, continuous horizontal rows rather than in two columns.

## Learning to think about an audience

As noted earlier in this book, writing differs from talking because the sender of the message and the receiver are usually separated from each other by time and space. Therefore we must make our messages clear when we write, and we must supply all of the needed information. Sophisticated writers serve as writer and reader as they write; that is, they move back and forth between the two roles.

Such mental flexibility requires advanced cognitive skills and experience. The writer understands that not everyone has had the same experiences, nor do they come away from similar experiences with the same ideas or information. Certainly we cannot expect preschool children to stand back from their writing and think about it in this way. However, we can use situations as they arise to help children begin to develop an awareness of audience.

Consider, for example, an activity in which one child is describing how to prepare peanut-butter-and-jelly sandwiches. The teacher is writing the directions on a piece of paper. The final version of the recipe will be drawn on a recipe chart to be used the following day when a small group of children will make peanut-butter-and-jelly sandwiches for snack. The child explains the process like this:

> "Well, first you take peanut butter and you put some on some bread. Then you push it around for a while. Then put jelly on some bread. That's all. Then you eat it."

The teacher then takes the opportunity to help the child think through his instructions from the standpoint of the children who will follow them:

> "OK," says the teacher, after writing all of the child's dictation down, "Let me see if I got this right. First you take peanut butter. Now, should that peanut butter be cold or room temperature?"
>
> "What?" asks the puzzled child.
>
> "Well, I'm wondering if the peanut butter should be cold and hard or warm and soft. It might be very hard to spread if it's cold. Where does your mom keep the peanut butter?"
>
> "In the cupboard."
>
> "Oh, then it would be room temperature; kind of warm."
>
> "Right."
>
> "Then you said that we should push the peanut butter around. Do you use something to push it with?"
>
> "Yes, I use a knife. Well, it isn't really a knife. It's not sharp. It's sort of a spreader thing."

"Well we could say, 'Spread the peanut butter on the bread with a dull knife or spreader.'"

"OK."

"Now, how do you decide when to stop spreading the peanut butter?"

"Well, you stop when it's all over the bread."

"I guess that's pretty obvious. Maybe we don't need to put that in."

"No, that's pretty easy."

"OK, then you said to put jelly on some bread. Do you mean that you spread jelly on a second slice of bread, just as you spread the peanut butter on the other slice?"

"Yes."

"OK. We can say, 'Spread jelly on a second slice of bread.' Then you said . . . no, you said that was it. But don't you have to put the two slices of bread together to make a sandwich?"

"Well, yes."

"Well, maybe we'd better say that. Some of the children who will be cooking may never have made sandwiches before. OK, we'll say, 'Place the slices of bread with jelly and peanut butter together to make a sandwich.' Then do you cut the whole thing into halves or fourths?"

"Sometimes, but you don't have to."

"Well, because our sandwiches are for snack instead of for lunch, we'd better cut them so they'll be small. Let's say, 'Cut into fourths.' OK?"

"OK."

"Now, let me read through all of this to see if we have it right. [Reads recipe.] How does that sound? Did we include everything?"

"Yes."

"OK. Thanks for going over this. I'll make a big chart for tomorrow."

In this situation the teacher helped the child think through his first dictation from the point of view of another child by acting as if she did not quite understand how the peanut-butter-and-jelly sandwiches were to be made. A naive reader might actually engage in this sort of questioning if she had requested a recipe and was somewhat unsure of the directions supplied. In the process, details taken for granted by the child were added by the writer of the recipe. In addition, a modification in the usual procedure was suggested (cutting the sandwiches into fourths) because the recipe was to be used to make sandwiches for snack.

The teacher in this example did a wonderful job of helping the child think about his audience, although she may not have thought of her actions in

> The most important thing we can do to support children's beginning efforts at writing is provide materials.

this way. The problem to be solved was a very practical one: a recipe needed to be formulated clearly. It just so happened that the teacher was eliciting recipes from the children, and because of children's inability to think of things from the point of view of others, the dictated recipes needed some rounding out, which is what the teacher helped the children do.

Teachers and parents might be able to think of a number of situations in which going over a child's dictation in this manner would make sense. This technique seems to work best when there is a real purpose for making the writing clearer. For example, a child who has dictated a story mostly for the pleasure of doing so should not be queried about possible missing details. In fact, if the child writes a story only for himself, there is no reason to try to think about another audience. However, if a child is relaying some personal experience orally at the snack table, for example, and the teacher thinks details are not clear to the other children, questions can prompt the child to provide information that is more coherent and detailed.

Because preschool children are just beginning to put their thoughts down on paper, they are occupied rather completely by just getting *anything* down. We need not bother a child in this situation about how the story would sound to someone else. We must use our good judgment here. On the other hand, if a child is dictating a thank-you note for a gift, some assistance may be needed to help the child express pleasure about it in a way that will be understood by the recipient.

## Supporting children's writing efforts

The most important thing we can do to support children's beginning efforts at writing is to provide materials. A writing center well supplied with paper and various writing tools belongs in every preschool classroom. This is a place where children can experiment with and explore writing and where they can go if they wish to write a message or create a story. Suggestions for organizing a writing center can be found in the box titled "Supplies for the Writing Center," although the materials might vary. Parents too can make materials available to children at home, perhaps in an area near the grocery list or at a desk where other family members routinely write letters or pay bills.

## The writing center

Because children often wish to make greeting cards or books; write notes, letters, or stories; or experiment with various writing materials, they need a place in the classroom for these activities. This area, like the literacy-skills materials area discussed earlier, need not be large. Because it will be available every day during the activity period, when children may choose between it and many other centers, space for three or four children to work comfortably is adequate. A table and several chairs, plus a shelf for storing writing materials, provide the basic setup for the area. Writing supplies can vary, but might include a selection of items such as those listed in the box below.

# *S*upplies for the Writing Center

Pencils (thin lead, #2 with eraser; thick lead without eraser; colored pencils; wax pencils if appropriate surfaces are available)

Markers (both wide- and fine-tipped, available in a variety of colors, all watercolor)

Magic slates and wooden pencils

Alphabet letter stamps and ink pads

Typewriter or computer with word processing

Paper (plain newsprint, white and colored construction paper, typing or mimeo paper, computer print-out paper)

Acetate sheets and wipe-off cloths

Letter and design stencils

Index and computer cards

Stapler

Hole punch

Scissors

Paste and glue stick

Pencil sharpener

Book of wallpaper samples for use as book covers

Stationery, perhaps created with stickers

Envelopes

Old magazines

Chalk and chalkboard

Bits of string and yarn

Of course, materials alone are not enough. Adults must interact with children to answer their questions and to offer information. There are times when questions intended to help children think about their writing are appropriate and helpful, even in preschool classrooms. The situation with the recipe is a good example of such an instance. But many times we can facilitate preschool children's writing development by providing materials and responding to their questions.

Preschool teachers should keep in mind that mistakes are essential in moving learning forward. As we saw earlier in this chapter, in the examples of children experimenting with letter writing (Figures 5-11, 5-12, and 5-13), children apparently make mistakes deliberately to gain a better understanding of how to make letters. While there are instances in which the characteristics of an error signal to adults that they might help by intervening directly—for example, when Claire wrote her name as a mirror image (Figure 5-18)—many errors are not of this kind and need no direct correction from an adult at the time they are made.

To understand the approach to children's early writing efforts that best supports them, their teachers might find it useful to think about how they consider children's behavior in creating with paint or blocks. Preschool teachers typically accept the ways children draw and build. They understand children's need to explore and experiment. A similar attitude of acceptance coupled with supporting development is also appropriate at the writing center.

Of course, the domain of literacy differs from the domain of art. Conventions must eventually guide much of our literacy behavior; we can take more liberties with art. Nevertheless, in the beginning stages writing and other aspects of literacy learning are nurtured when children are given opportunities to explore and discover. It is not an either-or situation. There are also opportunities to help children move forward. Teachers both notice and create these opportunities in some of the ways we have described here.

## References

Adams, M.J. 1990. *Beginning to read.* Cambridge, MA: MIT Press.

Baghban, M. 1984. *Our daughter learns to read and write.* Newark: DE: International Reading Association.

Berk, L. 1996. *Infants and children: Prenatal through early childhood.* 2d ed. Boston: Allyn & Bacon.

Bissex, G.L. 1980. GYNS AT WRK: A child learns to write and read. Cambridge, MA: Harvard University Press.

Carlson, K., & J.L. Cunningham. 1990. Effects of pencil diameter on the grapho-motor skills of preschoolers. *Early Childhood Research Quarterly* 5: 279–93.

Clay, M. 1975. *What did I write?* Portsmouth, NH: Heinemann.

Ferreiro, E., & A. Teberosky. 1982. *Literacy before schooling.* Trans. by K.G. Castro. Portsmouth, NH: Heinemann.

Gardner, H. 1980. *Artful scribbles: The significance of children's drawings.* New York: Basic Books.

Gibson, E. J. 1975. Theory-based research on reading and its implications for instruction. In *Toward a literate society,* eds. J.B. Carroll & J.S. Chall. New York: McGraw-Hill.

Harste, J.C., C.L. Burke, & V.A. Woodward. 1981. Children, their language and world: Initial encounters with print. Final report of the National Institute of Education Project # NIE-G-79-0132. Indiana University, Bloomington.

Holland, P.A. 1982. Developing an awareness of written language. Mimeographed.

Lavine, L. 1977. Differentiation of letter-like forms in prereading children. *Developmental Psychology,* 13 (2): 89–94.

Liberman, I., D. Shankweiler, F.W. Fischer, & B. Carter. 1974. Explicit syllable and phoneme segmentation in the young child. *Journal of Experiemental Child Psychology* 18: 201–12.

Menyuk, P. 1976. Relations between acquisition of phonology and reading. In *Aspects of reading acquisition,* ed. J.T. Guthrie. Baltimore, MD: Johns Hopkins University Press.

Papandropoulou, I., & H. Sinclair. 1974. What's a word? Experimental study of children's ideas on grammar. *Human Development* 17: 241–58.

Read, C. 1975. Children's categorization of speech sounds in English. Urbana, IL: National Council of Teachers of English.

Rich, S.J. 1985. The writing suitcase. *Young Children* 40 (5): 42–44.

Schickedanz, J.A. 1990. *Adam's righting revolutions: One child's literacy development from infancy through grade one.* Portsmouth, NH: Heinemann.

Schickedanz, J.A., & J. Hultz. 1979. Boston University Preelementary Reading Improvement Project. U.S. Office of Education Grant No. G007-605-403. Unpublished data.

Schickedanz, J.A., & A. Molina. 1979. Boston University Preelementary Reading Improvement Project. U.S. Office of Education Grant No. G007-605-403. Unpublished data.

Schickedanz, J.A., & M. Sullivan. 1984. Mom, what does u-f-f spell? *Language Arts* 61 (1): 7–17.

Schickedanz, J.A., & B. Waldorf. 1980. Boston University Preelementary Reading Improvement Project. U.S. Office of Education Grant No. G007-605-403. Unpublished data.

Stahl, S.A., A.M. Duffy-Hester, & K.A.D. Stahl. 1998. Everything you wanted to know about phonics (but were afraid to ask). *Reading Research Quarterly* 33 (3): 338–55.

Taylor, I. 1981. Writing systems and reading. In *Reading research: Advances in theory and practice, volume 2,* eds. G.E. MacKinnon & T.G. Waller. New York: Academic.

When adults thoughtfully plan children's environments and activities to incorporate literacy, reading and writing are meaningful in children's everyday lives.

# *Organizing the Environment to Support Literacy Development*

T hose who have studied literacy experiences in children's homes have found that they pop up all the time. People use written language to get things done (Taylor 1983; Schickedanz & Sullivan 1984; Teale 1986; Taylor & Dorsey-Gaines 1988; Schickedanz 1990). Grocery lists are written, boxes are labeled in preparation for a move to a new house, letters are opened and read, checks are written, recipes are followed, phone messages are taken, the calendar is consulted to check appointments, homework is completed, the oven and washing machine dials are set.

Amid all of this activity, young children serve as helpers, and they play. When helping, they are typically given a little bit to do and are helped to do it. If children help cook, the parent might read both the name of the next ingredient and the amount specified. Then the parent helps the child locate the container with the appropriate name, perhaps by saying, "'Vanilla' starts with /vvvv/ *v*. Let's see now. The word on that container starts with *s*, for *salt*. The word on that bottle starts with *r*, for *red* food coloring. Oh, here we go. This word starts with *v*. *Va-nill-a*. We need half a teaspoon. You hold the spoon and I'll pour." Or a child might be helped to add an item to the family grocery list. The parent might sound out the word and also help the child determine which letters are needed to represent each sound.

Families also provide materials for the purpose of children's entertainment and education, as well as to help with daily routines and difficult times. Games, toys, books, paper and pencil, paint, and playdough provide hours of enjoyment. Books ease the child into bedtime; books and paper and pencil help pass the time during a car or plane ride, and they can make waiting in the doctor's office a little more tolerable.

These experiences with literacy are evident in children's play, and in play we see children further explore and elaborate their understandings of print and its functions. They use their toy dishes and empty food containers to pretend that they are cooking. If recipes or cookbooks are provided, they are likely to incorporate these props into their play. If paper and a pencil are provided, a child who has helped with the family grocery list will probably make lists as part of grocery store pretend play. A child may comfort a sick baby doll by reading him a book while waiting to see the doctor. A doll

In play, children further explore and elaborate their understandings of print and its functions.

is instructed in how to spell her name using the child's set of magnetic alphabet letters and then is helped to complete the child's own alphabet puzzle.

Opportunities for literacy learning should abound in a preschool classroom, just as they do in many homes. The goal is to make them an integral part of classroom life. This means that children use written language in the normal course of each day as they find and use materials, as they make transitions from one time of the day to the next, as they help out with classroom chores and maintenance, and as they play.

This chapter discusses how to create preschool classroom environments in which literacy resources are provided to children and literacy is used throughout the day by children and adults. The chapter is organized in sections pertaining to different types of literacy experiences. There are literacy experiences relating to the overall physical arrangement of the classroom and to classroom routines, and there are those relating to the material resources a teacher provides for literacy learning in classroom activity areas. Parents can select and adapt some of these suggestions for use at home with their preschool-age child.

## Using print to organize the preschool classroom

When an early childhood classroom is well organized, everything tends to run more smoothly. The physical environment should be arranged and kept in good order, and the day should be arranged in terms of a schedule of activities. Labels, lists, signs, and charts can help us to organize the environment and the children's activities while providing, at the same time, many meaningful print experiences for the children.

### *Labels and signs*

Every room for young children requires at least a few labels. Cubbies should be labeled with children's names so that everyone knows whose cubby is whose. There is no need to place a picture of an animal or an object alongside the name, even for younger children. The name will stay in the same position on the cubby throughout the year, which will help even a very young child find her cubby after being assisted only a time or two. Children's names can be written in conventional form, with an uppercase letter at the beginning, followed by lowercase letters. Although children find it easier at first to *write* uppercase rather than lowercase letters, the print they see in books and other contexts contains both upper- and lowercase letters. Exposure to conventional print on name labels helps children get accustomed to the print they see in much of their world.

> **Involvement in arranging materials and attaching labels to the shelves or bins helps children notice the labels and understand their purpose.**

Labels are useful also to indicate where in the room various materials are kept. If containers of materials belong in specific places on shelves, both the containers and the shelves can be marked with matching labels. A picture of the item can be included on the label, along with the print, given the number of items in need of labeling. Unlike a cubby situation, in which a child must learn the location of only his or her own hook and cubby drawer, the items on classroom shelves can be numerous.

Because teachers cannot be everywhere at cleanup time, pictures to accompany the print on labels help. Children need some assistance at first to learn that materials are to be returned to a specific shelf, or place on a shelf, and that labels on the containers and shelves match. Children may not appreciate the purpose of the labels, and they may ignore them unless teachers explain the entire setup. Then, as children are in the process of putting items away, teachers also can help and remind them to find the two labels that match.

One way to help 4- and 5-year-olds become aware of labels and their function is by helping to prepare the labels and attach them to containers and shelves. Using the computer printer ahead of time, teachers can print out the necessary labels and then ask children who are interested to help place them in the appropriate places. Children can decide where various items might best be placed. Involvement in arranging materials and attaching labels to the shelves or bins helps children notice the labels and understand their purpose.

In addition to labels, many early childhood classrooms need the help of signs or notices. A Quiet Please sign might be placed in the library corner. A picture of a face with the letters *sh-sh-sh-sh* coming from the mouth might help children remember what the notice says. Signs can be useful when it is necessary to limit the number of children who may occupy an area in the classroom. For example, it may be safe for only two children at a time to work in the woodworking area. A sign saying Two Children Only could be posted, and a picture of two children pasted or drawn beside the print.

Many other signs may be useful. If routine directions are given in a particular place, a notice or sign might be considered. These can range from signs reading Wash Your Hands, Please and Flush the Toilet, Please posted in the bathroom to Walk, Please or Watch Your Step, Please signs in a hallway or on the wall next to stairs.

As with labels, children's involvement in the creation of notices is likely to increase their awareness of their content. Teachers may want to write the message and then have children decorate around the print. This way the sign is readable and serves as an appropriate example of writing for children, but children are still involved in making it.

Plants grown in a science area might be labeled Marigolds, Beans, Coleus. Or a sign could be made for a fish tank to give the names of the fish. Such a sign could be in the form of an activity card:

Can you find the *catfish?*

Can you find the *snails?*

Can you find the *guppies?*

A magnifying glass near the fish tank will encourage children to search. Pictures of each fish, perhaps cut out from a magazine and pasted on the sign, help the children know what they are looking for.

### Charts

Charts are lists or summaries of information. These too are needed in preschool classrooms.

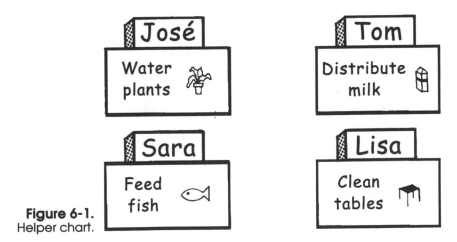

**Figure 6-1.**
Helper chart.

**Helper and attendance charts.** Helper charts post jobs that need to be done and the names of the children who are assigned to do them. A helper chart might look like the one in Figure 6-1.

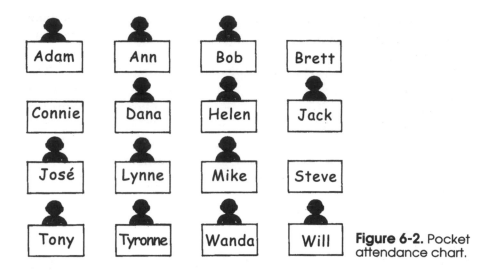

**Figure 6-2.** Pocket attendance chart.

When jobs are assigned or selected on a daily basis rather than weekly, children have more opportunities to use a helper chart. Teachers may be surprised at how quickly children learn to recognize their own names, as well as the names of their classmates, from a chart of this kind.

Teachers may also wish to use an attendance chart. Young children often enjoy pocket charts like the one shown in Figure 6-2. In some classrooms, jobs are posted on the attendance chart pockets. Velcro attached to each of the children's name pockets and to the back of job notices makes this approach work.

Combining attendance and helper charts in this way can reduce the wall space a teacher must devote to charts. It also gives the attendance chart a meaningful purpose, which is important in the preschool classroom. Children assigned the task of determining how many cartons of milk are needed for snack or lunch for the day can use the chart, counting the number of name tags in the attendance chart pockets. The attendance chart can be used in other ways as well. At a morning meeting, the teacher can point out the names of children who are absent and explain why. Children usually are interested in knowing if other children are sick or if they are absent for some other reason.

When constructing an attendance chart, the teacher can organize names alphabetically, giving children an opportunity to observe this organizational system. As with so many other things children learn, very little needs to be said explicitly about alphabetical order. Children will gain an intuitive understanding of it as they use the chart. From time to time there may be opportunities for a teacher to comment specifically about it. For example, as children put their name tags in their pocket on the chart when they arrive each day, the teacher can say, "Yes, that's where your pocket is. Your name starts with the letter *A,* and the *A* names are together here at the beginning of the top row."

Children sometimes find it difficult to locate their own name tag among a large assortment of tags. Teachers may want to use a flat box lid to lay out the names randomly in rows. Children soon learn what letter their name begins with and who else's name begins with that letter. They use this information to find their name.

In the case of the loose name tags, it is more instructional if teachers do not arrange them in the same order each day. If a stable order is maintained, children merely learn a position, grab their name tag, and put it in the appropriate pocket of the attendance chart without even looking at the print. If children do not know exactly where among the name tags their own tag is each day, they scrutinize the print to find it. (Children's pictures need not be put with the printed name; children will soon learn to recognize it by the print features.)

Daily engagement with name tags provides a good opportunity for children to learn about written words. For example, a teacher can sometimes be there to say, "Yes, that tag says *Victoria,* V-i-c-t-o-r-i-a," while pointing to the letters in the name. Or a teacher may say, "Yes, that is your name, Oliver. You know, your name has a *v* in the middle, and Victoria's name has a *v* at the beginning. Nobody else in our class has a *v* in their name."

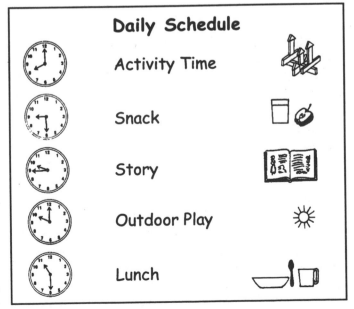

**Figure 6-3.**
Daily schedule.

**Daily schedule and calendar charts.** A third kind of chart that may be used to bolster literacy learning is one displaying the daily schedule (Figure 6-3). When a child asks, "When do we go outside?" the teacher can refer to the chart as he explains, "First we have snack, then we have story, and then we go outside." Or if a visitor or a new volunteer is in the classroom, children can be asked to review the daily schedule with her so she will know what the school day is like.

In addition to the daily schedule chart, a calendar can also be useful. A calendar takes on meaning when children's birthdays, school holidays, and other important events are posted on it. If calendars are used to help children see how many days it is until a birthday or a class field trip, then children can begin to appreciate a calendar's usefulness and to understand its structure.

The primary reason for having a classroom calender is to give children a tool to understand the timing of events. A calendar in a preschool classroom is not used to teach time concepts or the structure of this time-measuring instrument. Time first begins to make sense to young children in terms of their own life. In the process of using a calendar as a reference tool, children learn a lot about the structure of calendars—probably much more than if days, months, and years are recited as a daily ritual. Pointing to a calendar at group time while reciting the day of the week, the date, the month, and the year has little meaning for young children. This ritual is one of the most dulling to young children because they simply cannot comprehend it.

If a calendar is designed so its parts (labels for days, weeks, months, and dates) are easily removed and rearranged, children can help create the calendar for each new month as it arrives. Velcro can be used to create a versatile calendar. This activity itself can involve much learning for children age 4½ or 5. If the names of the months are stored in a box, children helping to change the calendar at the start of a new month can search for the label for that month. The labels for the days of the week will stay in the same place, of course, but the numerals usually must be moved around to create the new month. These too can be laminated and backed with Velcro to make rearrangement easy.

It is sometimes helpful to have children post the first few numerals of a new month at the end of the previous month to fill in the remaining days of the week. In this way they can see why the first day of the next month may not fall on a Sunday or Monday. Children often want to begin the new month on the first day of the week. If the teacher can help them see that the "old" month already used up those days, children begin to get the idea of how calendars work.

Special tags can be created to indicate special days. For example, a pumpkin tag may be created to put on October 31. Birthday cake tags with children's names written on them can indicate birthdays. School vacation days may have tags that say Vacation. These are then attached to the appropriate dates, again with a small bit of Velcro tape.

**Recipe charts.** When children cook, they can use a recipe chart. These large, attractive displays of the recipe make it easy for children to follow along, with an adult's guidance. Some teachers prefer smaller charts with one step posted on each page. When the pages are gathered together in a ring binder, a large book with a recipe is the result.

## *Lists*

Lists can also be used to support classroom organization. For example, if a new activity or new equipment is available in the classroom, chances are that many children will want a turn during the first few days. One way to resolve fairly the problem of activity overload is to make a name list for turn taking. This solution also provides an opportunity to demonstrate to children another function of written language—helping us remember and keep track of things.

Children can participate most fully in using a turn-taking list when the teacher invites them to write their own name and refers them to the name list when they ask, "When will it be *my* turn?" The teacher can point and say, "Let's see. Helen is using the typewriter now. Then John gets a turn. Tyronne's name comes next, and your name follows his. It might be afternoon before you can have your turn. While you wait, you might like to paint or look at books. When Tyronne is finished with his turn, I will let you know that it is your turn." After children have taken their turn, they can cross their name off the list and see whose name appears next. The teacher may need to help children read the next name, especially if children have written their names themselves.

Other lists might include a shopping list for supplies for snack preparation, a list of favorite parts of a field trip, a list of steps to take when engaging in an activity or using a special piece of equipment, a list of items to take along on a walk, or a list of foods to try. There are countless ways teachers and children can incorporate their planning and summarize meaningful events using lists.

### Summary

We have considered a variety of ideas for using print in routine situations to help organize the classroom environment. They are excellent ways to help children develop literacy knowledge because print used for a purpose is meaningful and functional. Moreover, the routine nature of these situations provides repeated encounters with print, which is important in helping children learn. Teachers and parents will marvel at the way children learn their own names and the names of classmates, as well as the content of signs and labels, from using charts, lists, and signs day after day.

## Using print in classroom activities

Print can be incorporated in many of children's activities. Miniature road signs can be included in the block area. If index cards, scissors, markers, and tape are also made available, children can make signs for buildings or for animal cages in a zoo they have created. Appropriate books with animal pictures and names make good resources for children.

Other classroom materials may also have print on them. For example, some of the play people figures are labeled. One woman transit worker's bus is labeled Bus, and a mail carrier's bag is labeled U.S. Mail. Some vehicles intended for use with blocks also have words printed on them. The same props, or similar ones, can be included in sand play when children are building roads, cities, or zoos.

Puzzles too can be selected for their print potential. Puzzles with road signs always contain print, and some occupation puzzles have labels such as School Crossing Guard or Police Officer. Storybook puzzles may incorporate the title of a nursery rhyme or story.

Picture lotto games often have the name of the object underneath the picture. Picture lotto games made by the teacher can easily be designed to have this print feature.

### Materials for specific literacy practice

Two children are playing with a deck of labeled picture cards. Each child draws one card from the deck, then turns it face up on the table. Suddenly, after the fourth or fifth round of turns, one child announces, "I have a pair! I have a pair! *Key* and *pea* rhyme!" He places these cards together, then sets them apart from the others on the table. The game continues.

In another area of the room, a child quickly finishes placing all the alphabet letters back in the wooden puzzle frame from which they were

> **Print can be incorporated into many of children's activities.**

dumped. And yet another child is matching letter tiles to their twin on a background board.

*   *   *

In these situations, print-related materials allow children to learn something about a specific aspect of literacy. Specific literacy materials isolate various skills, separating them from a meaningful context in which the skill would be used functionally. These types of experiences should not be the only ones in a preschool or kindergarten classroom, nor should their use dominate children's time. However, children love to practice and master various skills, be they physical skills—such as successfully using scissors to cut a piece of paper—or languages skills—entertaining adults with "knock-knock" jokes or nonsense words that rhyme.

As long as children have many authentic literacy experiences—experiences in which literacy is used for a purpose and all of its various aspects are brought together in the acts of reading and writing—some use of specific practice materials will do no harm. In fact, they provide an opportunity for children to do something they like: repeat a skill or action over and over until they master it.

The important thing to remember is that literacy-skill play should take place within a larger context of meaningful written language. While the children may be *physically* isolated from this larger context at certain times, no psychological isolation need exist because children bring the larger context they have gained from experience to any episode of isolated skill play; and they take back to contextually based experiences any new insights gained from skill play.

### *Alphabet-learning materials*

Alphabet learning is an appropriate goal for preschool and kindergarten children, although certain methods of approaching this learning are *not* appropriate. "Teaching the alphabet" includes more than helping children learn to distinguish the letters and name them. It also includes helping children know how alphabet letters function in written language.

# *T*eaching about the Alphabet in Authentic Contexts

Children at a table in a preschool classroom worked busily with puzzles and other manipulatives. One child had selected a road-sign puzzle from the collection of puzzles provided on the shelf. As he placed the stop sign in the correct space in the puzzle frame, he said to a nearby teacher, "Hey, this is a stop sign!" "It sure is," responded the teacher, as she pointed to the letters on the stop sign. "S-T-O-P," she said. "That spells *ssstooopppp.*"

Soon one of the children at the writing-and-drawing table across the room called to the teacher, "Miss Blaney, I want to write Michaela's name, and I can't find it." The teacher moved to the writing-and-drawing table and began to straighten up the set of name cards the child had been searching through. "Let's get these all gathered together," she said as she organized them in the ring binder. "Okay, now let's look for Michaela's name. This name starts with a *J*. It is Joe's name, not Michaela's. And here's a name starting with *B*. It says *Ben*. And here's Chuck's name, with the *ch* at the beginning."

They searched past a few more name cards, with the teacher naming the first letter of each name before identifying whose it was. "Oh, here's a name that might be Michaela's. It starts with an *M* . . . *Mmmiiichaaaelaaa*. Yes, this is it. I'll set it right here if you'd like to copy it onto your envelope. Mmmmm, that envelope is rather fat. Is there something inside it for Michaela?"

"Yes, a picture," the child replied.

*   *   *

The first child in the scenario above had set out to work on a puzzle and the second child was searching for a friend's name. Neither was trying to learn the names of alphabet letters. Yet the teacher found ways to include alphabet learning as she responded to each child.

## The importance of alphabet learning

"Learning the alphabet" is an essential part of early learning about literacy. Letter name knowledge is a very good predictor of success in beginning reading (Ehri & Sweet 1991; Chall 1996). Distinguishing between letters and learning their names is not all there is to "learning the alphabet." Knowing how alphabet letters function in writing and knowing specific letter-sound associations are crucial. Otherwise, children cannot use the letter-name knowledge they have.

Teachers can provide a range of activities to help children learn about the alphabet. Some of this learning can take place in the context of broad experiences. Other opportunities for learning can be provided through specific alphabet materials such as puzzles and matching games. If specific alphabet materials are just one part of a total literacy program, children will enjoy using these materials because they will know to which experiences in the world they relate. It is only when alphabet teaching takes place in a narrow, linear, "skills-first" program that children find learning about the alphabet tedious and meaningless. This can happen, for example, if the language arts or reading program consists of studying one letter each week for an entire preschool or kindergarten school year, or of writing one letter repeatedly each day, on a workbook page. However, there is no need to approach alphabet learning in these ways; many better options exist.

Specific alphabet materials such as those described in this section need not be excluded from preschool and kindergarten programs simply because they are not functional or authentic literacy activities. Children enjoy practicing a specific part of a larger task in order to become more skilled. If many authentic and functional literacy activities are provided in a program, specific alphabet materials will not seem abstract and meaningless to the child, nor will their use constitute isolated, decontextualized instruction. (See "Teaching about the Alphabet in Authentic Contexts" on pages 146–47.) Children using these specifically focused materials will incorporate the broader literacy understandings they've gained from experiences with authentic, functional activities.

**Alphabet manipulatives.** Alphabet puzzles, alphabet matching games, and other print-related manipulatives can be included on the shelves in a preschool classroom. Alphabet puzzles may be uppercase and lowercase. Matching games can include those in which upper- and lowercase letters are to be matched with one another and those in which similar-looking letters are to be discriminated. For the latter, teachers can put five or six easily confused letters in the left-hand column on a background piece of tagboard and then make a set of tagboard tiles for matching with each of these letters. The tile twins are placed in the right-hand column. Lamination helps these materials survive extensive handling. Velcro dots on the back of the tiles and down the two columns on the board hold the tiles in place effectively.

In this age of computer printers, alphabet matching games can include matching the same letter printed in different fonts. Or a sorting activity might include putting together letters with similar distinctive features. For example, one category label might comprise letters with straight, horizontal, and vertical lines; and another category might comprise letters with curved lines only or letters with diagonal lines. These matching and sorting activities help children learn to distinguish groups of letters from other letters, based on certain features.

A print-related manipulative might focus on the line segments found in specific letters. For example, *T, H, I, L, E,* and *F* are printed in the left-hand column of a piece of tagboard, and small tiles with line segments are supplied. The tile intended as the match for the *T* would have a long vertical line and a shorter horizontal line. The tile to match the *H* would include two long vertical lines and one short horizontal line. A letter with its line-matches printed at the top of the tagboard card would show children how to play with this manipulative.

Other print-related manipulatives might include labeled picture cards of animals or fruits or vegetables, for example, with several pictures making a set. The letters needed to recreate the labels on the pictures would be provided. Print-related manipulatives can also include picture-letter matching materials. Two or three pictures of objects with names beginning with the same consonant phoneme are clustered together on a background board. Alphabet letters are provided for matching with the picture clusters. Children name the pictures and isolate the first phoneme. They decide which alphabet letter would typically be used to represent this phoneme, and they find it among the letter tiles provided. A variety of these picture-letter match materials can be made and rotated through the classroom during the year, perhaps in connection with specific units of study.

**Alphabet books.** Because alphabet books do not contain stories, they are not especially suitable for reading at story time. Yet, many alphabet books are intriguing and delightful in their own way! If a number of them are placed in the classroom library corner, teachers and classroom volunteers can read them to individuals or small groups of children who gather in the book area. (See the list of alphabet books at the end of Chapter 3.)

A typical alphabet book follows a format in which a letter is introduced on each page, along with pictures of objects whose names begin with the phoneme represented by the letter. Because of this format, alphabet books not only help children learn to identify and name alphabet letters, they introduce them to letter-sound associations in the context of words. This approach provides experience in isolating a phoneme at the beginning of words, which helps children start to acquire skill in phonemic segmentation (Murray, Stahl, & Ivey 1996; Stahl, Duffy-Hester, & Stahl 1998). It also helps children learn specific letter-sound associations.

When we "help children learn the alphabet," we must be careful to include letter-sound association and phonemic awareness. Alphabet letters represent phonemes. Learning to distinguish between letters and to name them is only a very small piece of alphabetic learning. The most critical understanding for young children to develop is that of the function of alphabet letters in writing. Alphabet books, as well as authentic writing experiences, help children learn the alphabet in this comprehensive way.

### Sound materials

This category includes materials that stress rhyming words as well as those asking children to select words on the basis of similar consonant sounds at either the beginning or the end of a word. Commercial materials of this kind usually contain several pairs of pictures whose names rhyme or whose beginning or ending sounds are the same. Decks of cards with pictures of a cake and a rake, a house and a mouse, and a bat and a hat are typical of the former, whereas decks containing pictures of a ball and a bat, a cat and a car, and a dog and a duck are characteristic of the latter.

Teachers can devise many variations of these basic materials. For example, teachers might divide a piece of construction paper into four or six sections and then label each section with a letter. Then, a deck of picture cards can be prepared. Several pictures in the set would have names beginning with each of the letters appearing in the section on the construction paper. Children sort the pictures and place them with the letter that codes the first sound in the picture's name.

### Word-making materials

Word-making materials may be sets of specially designed alphabet letters. The individual pieces are typically smaller than those found in magnetic letter sets, for example, and all letters (especially the common vowels) are available in multiples. The letters from a Scrabble game serve nicely here, and there are other commercial materials of this kind in both wood and plastic. Teachers can make their own sets, of course, with tagboard, which can be laminated.

When providing sets of letters for children to use, the teacher needs to devise some way to organize the letters; otherwise, children may become frustrated while trying to find letters they need. Teachers can section off areas of a box lid using strips of tagboard, or they may find liners from cookie or candy boxes that already have been formed into sections. Each section can hold as many as three or four different letters. Children will still need to search for the letters they want, but the task is simplified considerably when letters are organized rather than thrown together in a box.

Other word-making materials children enjoy include flip cards that leave the root of a word the same while the initial letter changes—a word might change from bat to cat, to rat, to mat. Dial-a-word and turn-a-word materials are similar, although their pieces turn rather than flip. Most comprehensive early childhood materials catalogs have a wide variety of these types of materials.

## Summary

In this chapter, as in others in this volume, many suggestions have been made for ways to surround young children with print and engage them in literacy activities. When parents and teachers plan children's environments and activities carefully so that literacy is an integral part of everything they do, then literacy learning becomes a meaningful part of children's everyday lives. When teachers deliberately create such an environment, there is no need to set aside time for formal lessons about reading and writing in the preschool classroom. Preschool children can learn about written language as opportunities for lessons arise in the course of their many activities.

## References

Chall, J.S. 1996. *Learning to read: The great debate.* Rev. ed. New York: McGraw-Hill.

Ehri, L.C., & J. Sweet 1991. Fingerpoint-reading of memorized text: What enables beginners to process the print? *Reading Research Quarterly* 26 (4): 443–62.

Murray, B.A., S.A. Stahl, & M.G. Ivey. 1996. Developing phoneme awareness through alphabet books. *Reading and Writing: An Interdisciplinary Journal* 8: 307–22.

Schickedanz, J. 1990. *Adam's righting revolutions.* Portsmouth, NH: Heinemann.

Schickedanz, J., & M. Sullivan. 1984. Mom, what does u-f-f spell? *Language Arts* 61 (1): 7–17.

Stahl, S.A., A.M. Duffy-Hester, & K.A.D. Stahl. 1998. Everything you wanted to know about phonics (but were afraid to ask). *Reading Research Quarterly* 33 (3): 338–55.

Taylor, D. 1983. *Family literacy: Young children learning to read and write.* Portsmouth, NH: Heinemann.

Taylor, D., & C. Dorsey-Gaines. 1988. *Growing up literate: Learning from inner-city families.* Portsmouth, NH: Heinemann.

Teale, W.H. 1986. Home background and young children's literacy development. In *Emergent Literacy,* eds. W.H. Teale & E. Sulzby, 173–206. Norwood, NJ: Ablex.

I n Harper Lee's 1960 novel *To Kill a Mockingbird*, the main character, Scout, recounts her first day of school. Miss Caroline, the first-grade teacher—a beginner "no more than twenty-one"—started the day by reading a story to the children. It was a story about cats who conversed with each other and visited a drugstore to enjoy chocolate malted mice. Scout relates that most of her classmates were squirming like worms by the story's end. She accounts for their inability to sit quietly by explaining that they had spent their earliest years working in the fields, chopping cotton, and taking care of animals. They were, in Scout's words, "immune to imaginative literature."

After reading the story, Miss Caroline printed the letters of the alphabet on the chalkboard and asked if anyone knew what they were. Scout explains that everyone knew what they were because practically everyone had been in first grade the year before. Having failed first grade that year, they had been sent back for more.

Miss Caroline called on Scout, who read the letters without a problem. Surprised, Miss Caroline had Scout read from the reading book *My First Reader* and then from the newspaper (the stock-market quotations). After discovering that Scout could read, Miss Caroline instructed her to tell her father to stop teaching her because it was sure to "interfere."

Scout was surprised to hear her father's contribution to her reading skill described as "teaching." She hadn't considered that Atticus had taught her to read. At the end of the day, he didn't have the time or energy to teach her: "Why, he's so tired at night he just sits in the living room and reads," she explained to her teacher.

Miss Caroline didn't believe Scout. She asked who had taught her to read, if not her father. Miss Caroline claimed that someone must have because no one is born knowing how to read. When Scout attempted to explain how she might, in fact, have been born reading, her teacher cut her off, accusing her of letting her imagination run away at the very least or perhaps even lying.

Scout realized the wisdom of apologizing to Miss Caroline but continued to think about her situation. "I never deliberately learned to read," she concluded. All Scout could remember were situations in which she had been placed since she had been a very little girl, contexts that gave her access to reading demonstrations such as those provided by her father.

In the long hours of church—was it then that I learned? I could not remember not being able to read hymns. . . . . I could not remember when the lines above Atticus's moving finger separated into words, but I had stared at them all the evenings in my memory, listening to the news of the day, Bills To Be Enacted into Laws, the diaries of Lorenzo Dow—anything Atticus happened to be reading when I crawled into his lap every night. Until I feared I would lose it, I never loved to read. One does not love breathing.*

Upon further reflection, Scout decided that their housekeeper Calpurnia had taught her the alphabet. Apparently, on rainy days Calpurnia kept the young Scout occupied with writing. She wrote the alphabet at the top of Scout's tablet, above a passage from the Bible, and set for her the task of copying the Bible passage. If her writing was done very well, Scout was rewarded with a butter-and-sugar sandwich.

Teachers today are more enlightened than Miss Caroline seems to have been and more grateful, I suspect, when they find a child whose literacy learning has been nurtured by adults. Teachers' greater worry now is that too many children entering their classrooms have not been held often enough on a lap from which they might learn about reading, either at home or in a preschool or kindergarten classroom. Laps are in short supply for many children, no matter where they turn.

Each of us wishes that every child could learn to read without effort and without any memory of exactly when. We also wish that all children would learn to read in ways that would lead them to consider reading a vital part of their lives, a part of their very being. We might wish that we could do better than settle, as we do, for children in our classrooms learning at least to love reading. This is no small accomplishment, to be sure. But, for Scout, reading was not something she merely loved; reading was so much a part of her life that she could no more imagine living without it than she could imagine living without breathing.

Those who are entrusted with the care and teaching of children in the early years, when life is just beginning, have a chance to shape not only the progress a child makes in acquiring the technical skills so vital to learning to read, but the child's basic attachment to reading as well. Both spheres of influence are of great importance. I hope that *Much More Than the ABCs* will help teachers and parents as they work to achieve with children these dual and complementary goals.

*Source: From Harper Lee, *To Kill a Mockingbird* (Philadelphia: Lippincott, 1960), 17–18.

# Appendix 1

## Helping Children Learn about Reading: A Word to Parents

Parents often think that children learn about reading in elementary school. The truth of the matter is that many children already know a lot about reading when they enter kindergarten because parents have been teaching their children about reading from the time the children were born.

The methods parents use to teach children reading differ from those typically used in elementary school. Parents help children learn about reading every day—when they take them to the grocery store or when they point out street signs, for example. This type of experience with print gives children a broad and meaningful introduction to reading. Reading really cannot be learned very well if we start only with lessons on isolated letters and sounds. If reading is to make sense to children, they must see how it is used in life.

Think how silly it would be to give a baby talking lessons, to make sounds out of context and then expect the baby to repeat these! The baby might learn to make sounds and say words, but might never learn to use words to communicate with others. While children enjoy playing with language, they need much more to learn how to read.

Children who become good readers have had many experiences with print during their early years. They probably have seen their parents reading for pleasure or to obtain information. Reading becomes a part of their lives long before elementary school. Even after children enter elementary school, families can provide a variety of experiences that will help children make the best of their activities in a larger group. Although schools may have capable and dedicated teachers, schools are by their very nature isolated from the larger world.

Children learn from everything they see and do—at home, at school, and everywhere else. Here are some ideas for families who want to help their children learn about reading.

# How parents can help

**Infants.** Talk to your baby–during bathtime, at play, when changing clothes or diapers, at feeding time. Language is the cornerstone of reading development.

Sing to your baby–children's songs, folk songs, gospel–anything that you enjoy.

Prop up a cardboard book for the 2- to 4-month-old baby in the crib or on the floor. Select books with simple, bright pictures.

Read or recite nursery rhymes to your baby.

Babies from 6 to 12 months will look at, chew, pound on, or toss books. Cardboard or cloth books can be part of a child's toy selection. Paper books can be reserved for lap reading times.

Name and point to the pictures in books when your baby seems interested.

After you have been naming pictures for a few weeks, begin asking questions: "Where's the teddy bear?" Soon your baby will bat at or put a finger on the picture of the teddy bear.

Babies can ask, "What is that?" by pointing to pictures and babbling. This question-and-answer game is fun and helps increase your baby's vocabulary.

Before the age of 1 year, most babies like to handle books more than they like to listen to you read. Your baby's behavior will make it clear which is more interesting at the time.

Babies who laugh and smile when you play Pat-a-Cake, Peek-a-Boo, or This Little Piggy are old enough to play these games.

When your baby is old enough to sit up easily in a grocery cart, give her or him small unbreakable items to hold, such as a little box of raisins or crackers. Talk with your baby about the box and what is inside.

If you go to a restaurant that uses paper placemats, point out the pictures on the placemat. Babies also enjoy holding plastic-covered menus.

Take your baby to the park, the zoo, the library, the store. Babies learn from everything they see.

Babies can sit on your lap, in an infant seat, or in a high chair while you write letters or make grocery lists. Talk to your baby about what you are doing. Offer toys to younger babies. Children from about age 1 can begin to use blunt writing instruments such as watercolor markers to write on their own paper.

Junk mail is ideal reading material for your baby while you read the other mail. Just make sure baby doesn't eat the mail!

At about 1 year of age children may begin to notice the letters on wooden blocks or other toys. Talk about the letters or words and what they mean.

**Toddlers.** Toddlers will continue to ask questions about pictures or print. You can help your toddler make the transition from "Dat?" or "Whassat?" to "What's that?" by repeating "What's that?" before answering the question.

Stories can be used occasionally to help a child make a transition between active play and more restful activities. Reading books at bedtime has been a favorite of children for generations.

Toddlers who have been read to since babyhood sometimes ask you to read their favorite books repeatedly. Sometimes you may want to encourage your toddler to read the book alone while you are close by to comment. Other times when you read together you may want to pause before a familiar word to give your child a chance to point to the picture or say the missing word. Rhyming books are a good way to introduce this game.

Toddlers love to write and draw. Shelf paper or discarded computer paper makes inexpensive large sheets. Offer wide- and thin-tipped watercolor markers to your child. Establish a place for drawing to help your toddler understand that walls are not for drawing on. Drawing materials should be kept out of the toddler's reach but offered often.

Children enjoy sticking magnetic letters on the refrigerator. Soon you can spell the child's name or the names of other family members. You can name the letters as you would any other object. Sometimes, just for fun, make your child's name and leave a few other letters as well. Ask your child to find her or his name. Increase the number of extra letters as the toddler's skills grow.

Take your child to the library or bookstore to choose books. Some libraries have story hours for toddlers.

Continue to encourage your child to write shopping lists with you. Give your child coupons for a few favorite grocery items, and ask her or him to show you the coupon for a specific item.

Expand your child's horizons by taking short trips to interesting new places—a street festival, a sheep-shearing—and talk about what is happening. Read posters or programs for the event. Before you go, prepare your child by discussing what you will do. Read about similar functions if possible.

Letters or thank-you notes drawn by toddlers may be treasured by friends and relatives. Be sure to read letters aloud when they arrive from others.

**Preschoolers.** Your child probably says familiar stories along with you by now, or perhaps insists on reading to you sometimes. If you skip a word while reading, you will surely be corrected. This is an extremely important step in learning about reading. Add some new books to your child's collection, of course, but keep reading old favorites.

At this age shopping is still a marvelous way to help your child see how print works. Preschoolers can select items from the shelf. Cooking together is a terrific way to demonstrate how reading can be used to follow a recipe. Children can assemble the ingredients, stir, and pour while you read the directions.

When eating out, read napkins, placemats, and other printed items with your child. Some of the games printed on placemats are for older children, but younger ones may enjoy drawing on the paper.

Take books with you on long rides or for times when you must wait quietly.

Play games such as Go Fish, Hi-Ho! Cherry-O, or picture dominoes. Read the directions aloud and point out print on the materials. Don't expect preschoolers to play games perfectly—they have different ideas about what it means to follow rules.

Children ages 4 or 5 may begin to ask about print in books. You also might want to call attention to the print by asking questions such as "Where does it say *Max* on the boat?" Books with labeled pictures make it possible for children to use their knowledge of pictures to read the words.

Help your child make greeting cards. Older children might want to copy some words or may ask for spellings. Give one letter at a time. Writing materials can now be made freely accessible to children. Typewriters or home computers might also be a way to encourage emerging writing skills.

Use magnetic or wooden letters to spell important words for your child. You might make a few cards with these words written on them so that the child can select letters to form the words.

**School-age children.** Continue to read to and with your child, especially at bedtime, even if your child has learned to read. You can read one page and then your child can read one page.

Regular trips to the library are still important. Many libraries issue cards to children who can write their own names.

Control the amount of TV that the family watches. Have a family quiet hour every night for reading, writing, or doing homework.

Purchase stationery or paper, pens, and stickers for making stationery so your child can write thank-you notes or make greeting cards.

Encourage story writing by listening to the stories your child writes. Typewriters or home computers are excellent aids for story writing.

Join in when your child tells jokes or riddles. Language play helps your child think about sounds, words, and meanings.

Play word games such as Scrabble or Boggle with your child. Purchase inexpensive books of crossword puzzles and other word games that are convenient for taking in the car.

# Books for parents

Butler, D. (1982). *Babies need books.* New York: Atheneum. Lots of good ideas and some strong opinions about how and what to read to very young children.

Butler, D. (1979). *Cushla and her books.* Boston: Horn Book. A case study of a child with a disability and how books played an important role from infancy.

Butler, D., & Clay, M. (1979). *Reading begins at home.* Exeter, NH: Heinemann. Sensible information about what reading really is. Provides many ideas for parents.

Chall, J.S. (1983). *Stages of reading development.* New York: McGraw Hill. A thorough description of each stage a child goes through in learning to read. Differentiates prereading from initial reading stage.

Clay, M. (1987). *Writing begins at home.* Portsmouth, NH: Heinemann.

Larrick, N. (1982). *A parent's guide to children's reading* (5th ed.). New York: Bantam Books. Good lists of books for children.

Rossi, M.J.M. (1982). *Read to me: Teach me.* Wauwatosa, WI: American Baby Books. Good descriptions of many books for children from birth to age 5.

Schickedanz, J. (1990). *Adam's righting revolutions: A case study of writing development from age one to age seven.* Portsmouth, NH: Heinemann.

Two literacy brochures—"Helping Children Learn About Reading" by Judith Schickedanz (reprinted, in part, in this appendix) and "Raising a Reader, Raising a Writer: How Parents Can Help" —are published by NAEYC. The cost is 50¢ for each brochure or $10 for 100. NAEYC brochure #520 and #530, respectively, can be ordered directly from the National Association for the Education of Young Children, 1509 16th Street, NW, Washington, DC 20036-1426; phone: 202-232-8777 or 800-424-2460.

# Appendix 2

## Learning to Read and Write: Developmentally Appropriate Practices for Young Children

### Excerpted from the Joint Position Statement of the International Reading Association and the National Association for the Education of Young Children

Learning to read and write is critical to a child's success in school and later in life. One of the best predictors of whether a child will function competently in school and go on to contribute actively in our increasingly literate society is the level to which the child progresses in reading and writing. Although reading and writing abilities continue to develop throughout the life span, the early childhood years—from birth through age eight—are the most important period for literacy development. It is for this reason that the International Reading Association (IRA) and the National Association for the Education of Young Children (NAEYC) joined together to formulate a position statement regarding early literacy development. The statement consists of a set of principles and recommendations for teaching practices and public policy.

The primary purpose of this position statement is to provide guidance to teachers of young children in schools and early childhood programs (including child care centers, preschools, and family child care homes) serving children from birth through age eight. By and large, the principles and practices suggested here also will be of interest to any adults who are in a position to influence a young child's learning and development—parents, grandparents, older siblings, tutors, and other community members.

Teachers work in schools or programs regulated by administrative policies as well as available resources. Therefore secondary audiences for this position statement are school principals and program administrators whose roles are critical in establishing a supportive climate for sound, developmentally appropriate teaching practices; and policymakers whose decisions determine whether adequate resources are available for high-quality early childhood education.

A great deal is known about how young children learn to read and write and how they can be helped toward literacy during the first five years of life. A great deal is known also about how to help children once compulsory schooling begins, whether in kindergarten or the primary grades. Based on a thorough review of the research, this document reflects the commitment of two major professional organizations to the goal of helping children learn to read well enough by the end of third grade so that they can read to learn in all curriculum areas. IRA and NAEYC are committed not only to helping young children learn to read and write but also to fostering and sustaining their interest and disposition to read and write for their own enjoyment, information, and communication.

First, the statement summarizes the current issues that are the impetus for this position; then it reviews what is known from research on young children's literacy development. This review of research as well as the collective wisdom and experience of IRA and NAEYC members provides the basis for a position statement about what constitutes developmentally appropriate practice in early literacy over the period of birth through age eight. The position concludes with recommendations for teaching practices and policies.

The full position statement, published in the NAEYC journal *Young Children*–July 1998 (vol. 53, no. 4, pp. 30–46), the IRA journal *The Reading Teacher*–October 1998, and the NAEYC book "Learning to Read and Write: Developmentally Appropriate Practices for Young Children"–in press, can also be found on NAEYCs Website at **http://www.naeyc.org**.

# Index

## Subjects

# Authors

Dickinson, D.K. 6, 29, 45, 47, 53, 56
Dorsey-Gaines, C. 135
Downey, D.M. 44
Duffy-Hester, A.M. 125, 149
Dunham, F. 4
Dunham, P.J. 4
Dunn, J. 26
Durant, C. 17
Durkin, D. x, 5, 6, 83

Ehri, L. 3, 44, 83, 147
Eilers, R.E. 4, 15, 17
El Konin, D.B. 62
Elbro, C. 63
Elley, W.B. 3, 45, 53
Epstein, J.N. 44, 45, 56

Falco, F.L. 56
Fantz, R.L. 12
Farrar, M.J. 17, 54
Fenson, L. 20
Fernald, A. 5
Ferreiro, E. 118
Fielding, L. 65
Fischel, J.E. 56
Fischer, F.W. 63, 116
Fivush, R. 25
Flood, J. 29
Forsyth, A.G. 18
Forsyth, P.D. 18
Fung, H. 25

Galda, L. 46
Gardner, H. 98, 99
Gibson, E.J. 99, 108
Goetz, E.M. 88, 91
Goodwin, D.K. 64
Goswami, U. 63
Goubet, N. 18, 26
Griffin, P. 2, 96

Haight, W. 3, 4
Halle, P. 17
Harste, J.C. 100, 101
Hart, B. 3, 4
Heath, S.B. 6
Herman, P.A. 45
Hiebert, E.H. 6
Hogan, L.E. 29
Holdaway, D. 57
Holland, P.A. 103, 106, 114
Hultz, J. 100
Huttenlocher, J. 3, 4

Ivey, M.G. 149

Kanosky, J. 66
Karniol, RO. 16
Kessen, W. 12
Lamme, L. 16
Lavine, L. 99
Leeds, S. 29

Leseman, P.P.M. 1
Levitt, A.G. 17
Liang, C. 25
Liberman, I.Y. 63, 116
Lonigan, C.J. 44, 45, 56
Lyons, R. 3, 4

Maclean, M. 63
Marsh, H.W. 44, 85
Mattingly, I.Q. 2
McCabe, A. 26, 82
Mclane, J.B. 6
McNamee, G.D. 6
Menyuk, P. 116
Middleton, D. 21
Miller, P.J. 25
Moerck, E.L 54
Molina, A. 102, 105, 113
Monker, J. 44
Morgan, J.L. 54
Morrow, L.M. 29, 88, 89, 94
Munn, P. 26
Murray, B.A. 149

Nagell, K. 17
Nagy, W.E. 45
Needham, A. 26
Ninio, A. 21

Oller, D.K. 4, 15, 17
Ottinger, J. 66

Packer, A. 16
Papandropoulou, I. 118
Pearson, P.D. 65
Pellegrini, A.D. 46
Pergontis, M.L. 66
Perlmutter, J.C. 46
Petersen, D.K. 63
Peterson, C.L. 26, 82
Pethick, S.J. 20
Pikulski, J.J. 44
Powell, W. 45
Price, E. 6

Radke-Yarrow, M. 26
Raphael, T.E. 6
Rawson, R.M. 88, 91
Read, C. 5, 6, 122, 123
Reznick, J.S. 20
Rhodes, L. 29
Ricard, R.J. 54
Risley, T. 4
Robbins, C. 3, 44
Ross, G. 21
Rossman, F. 85

Salapatek, P. 12
Sagartt, L. 17
Schickedanz, D. 18
Schickedanz, J.A. 5, 6, 18, 29, 66, 98, 100, 101, 102, 103, 104, 105, 107, 109, 113, 118, 133

Schieffelin, B.M. 5
Scollon, B.K. 6
Scollon, R. 6
Seltzer, M. 3, 4
Senechal, M. 44
Shankweiler, D. 63, 116
Sheppard, L.J. 44
Sheppard, M.J. 44
Sinclair, H. 118
Smith, M.W. 6, 29, 47, 53, 56
Snow, C.E. 2, 13, 15, 54, 96
Snyder, L.S. 44
Spear-Swerling, L. 2
Sperry, D.E. 25
Sperry, L.L. 25
Stahl, K.A.D. 125, 149
Stahl, S.A. 125, 149
Steffens, M.L. 4, 17
Stein, N.L. 57
Sternberg, R.J. 2, 45
Strickland, D. 29
Sullivan, M. 5, 104, 105, 107, 135
Sulzby, E. 79, 80, 81
Sweet 83, 147

Tabors, P.O. 45
Taylor, D. 29, 86, 135
Taylor, I. 116
Teale, W.H. 5, 6, 135
Teberosky, A. 118
Thal, D.J. 20
Thomas, E. 44
Tobin, A.W. 44
Tomasello, M. 17
Travis, L.L. 54

Urbano, R. 4, 17

Valdez-Menchoca, M.C. 56

Wagner, E. 26
Waldorf, B. 104
Wang, Q. 17
Wells, G. 3, 44, 54
Whitehurst, G.J. 44, 45, 56
Whitney, P. 65
Wiley, A.R. 25
Wood, D.J. 21
Woodward, V.A. 100, 101

Yopp, H.K. 63

Zahn-Wexler, C. 26